FOR THE GRANDS AND THE GREATS
(A young-old man's story)

By: John Sterling Bridges

For the Grands and the Greats
By: John Sterling Bridges

ISBN-13: 978-1539329558
ISBN-10: 1539329550

CONTENTS

Contents

FORWARD

A few years ago Lorrie, my bride of 36 years, wrote a book called "Wet Mittens". It was a collection of short stories about life lessons she had learned. I adored her book and ever since its publication, I have been thinking about writing something similar. I often said, "When I grow up (meaning when I retire), maybe I'll do something like that!" Although I knew anecdotes from my life wouldn't necessarily provide any particular value to others, I nevertheless thought retelling a few select stories might at least be somewhat interesting and/or entertaining for future generations of our family … so … why not?

I've been telling stories my whole life, and as I get older they seem to get better (at least in my estimation) and longer (to the chagrin of my listeners). Yep, give me a rocking chair, a glass of wine, and an audience and I can spin a yarn with the best of them. "Shaggy dog stories" is what my dad would call them. At my dad's memorial service in 2015 his stories were a primary focus of the memories shared by family and friends alike. A good story is at the heart of history. Oral tradition has been important through the ages, and I think we are all the richer for it. But, putting a story down on paper, now that is not as easy as you might think. It can be difficult to emphasize feelings, accentuate key moments and portray emotion on paper. But then I've never been particularly dissuaded by difficult.

What finally moved me to write this was an excerpt I read from a short book my Grandma Bridges wrote called "Yesteryear". In it she shared tales from her years as a wife, mother and school teacher on the Outer Banks of North Carolina. As I enjoyed being swept away to a time long ago and a place far away, I was struck by a paragraph in which she spoke of me. She was immensely proud of her first-born grandson and her fervent prayer for me was that I would grow up to serve God. What? She had faithfully prayed for me all those years ago, and I never knew. She never mentioned it to me, even after I became a Christian, but there it was, in her book. Had she not written those words I would not have known about the spiritual legacy passed on to me through her. I was profoundly moved.

We need to tell our stories for the next generations. We need to leave written "monuments" for the children that they might learn and benefit from the mountains we've climbed, the valleys we've struggled through and the green pastures we've experienced. It's not really about us … it's about them.

I have been blessed with an amazing family and wonderful friends, many of whom are integral parts of my stories. I am also exceedingly blessed to know God. His work in and through my life has given rise to the most important reason to pass on my tales. I hope that someday, when I do finally grow up and become an "old-old" man, my grandchildren (and maybe even some "greats") will enjoy reading my tales and perhaps be intrigued enough to want to know God as I do.

Of course, it is always difficult to follow in someone else's wake. "Yesteryear" was a truly enchanting title. Lorrie's book title, "Wet Mittens", is perhaps one of the best I've ever seen. It is both pithy and provocative. It grabs your imagination and prompts you to delve in to discover the hidden treasure behind the words. Suffice it to say I would never attempt to compete with such a great book title. Perhaps seeking some remote connection to Lorrie's coat tails, I joked about calling this little anthology, "Leather Gloves." I thought maybe I could tie in some story about rose gardening or baseball (both of which necessitate such) but decided such an attempt might fall so flat as to relegate my work to the shelf even before the binding was cracked.

What then to call this odd collection of musings? Lorrie had been so certain (and correct) that a good title can mean everything for a book. Of course, for this story, not much more than a family memoir, the perfect title probably doesn't matter all that much, so I opted for something simple and to the point: "For the Grands and the Greats (a young-old man's story)". Yep, that would work just fine.

CHAPTER 1 - FORKS IN THE ROAD

As we travel down the path of life, sometimes we reach a fork in the road. Where each fork will lead is unknown. All that is certain is that once a path is chosen the other is likely to disappear forever. Great trepidation can arise when such a fork is approached. Fortunately, for the Christian, we can turn to God for guidance at such times. But such turns can raise interesting questions. How does one ask for direction? What does one listen for in terms of an answer? How is man's free will reconciled with Divine direction? The mystery of these questions notwithstanding, I have reached several such forks along my path and can look back in confidence regarding the choices I've made because of God's involvement in my decisions.

There is a story in the Bible about a man named Gideon who was unsure about how to proceed at a fork in the road. Gideon decided to seek God's direction by praying very specifically. He sought God's input by setting out a woolen fleece and asking that God rain only on the fleece if he were to pursue a particular path. God did so. Gideon then made a second request, this time asking God to rain everywhere except on the fleece. God did so. Through this exchange of specific petitions and answers, Gideon gained confidence to proceed down a particular path, even though that path seemed daunting at the time.

Since I wouldn't presume God would necessarily intervene every time I asked for direction, to be honest I haven't gone there very often. But on a few occasions, when the alternate paths before me were dramatically different and involved mountains I could never climb on my own, I have resorted to seeking Divine direction. I've never actually used sheep's wool, but I have prayed specifically. I believe God hears our prayers and that, in accordance with His will, He can (and at times does) choose to answer our prayers in a manner we can clearly comprehend. I can testify to this happening in a significant way at least twice in my walk with God, and in each case my future was altered in a dramatic way … as was my faith.

When Lorrie and I were in college we started a Christian gospel band called Hosanna. We were five young and energetic evangelists who wanted to spread the good news of the Gospel of Christ through song. I was the principal songwriter in the group, and though not a particularly accomplished musician, I also played keyboard and rhythm guitar. Lorrie was our lead female vocalist. We rehearsed with the group for hours every week and performed on weekends at churches and camps around the state of Montana. It was an absolute joy to serve God in this way.

During my senior year in college we booked an eight week concert tour for the summer following graduation. Before we left on tour, the group decided to create a "demo tape" of a few of our original songs and send it off to three Christian record companies. The hope was to land a record deal and thereby be able to make a career out of our ministry. We devoted many long weeks to producing that demo tape and we prayed over it constantly. We also agreed to set out a fleece to God regarding our long-term future as a band. We prayed very specifically that God would show us our future path by the response from the record companies. We prayed we could make a record together and thereby continue ministering as "Hosanna Band".

The concerts were wonderful but the travel was hard: five band members and a sound man in a single borrowed van with a homemade trailer hitched behind it to carry our instruments and sound equipment. We were our own roadies. We received a good will offering at the end of each concert, hoping to get enough money to pay for gas to the next town and maybe lunch along the way. We weren't too concerned about money because we knew the local churches wouldn't let us starve … but as the tour drew to an end we all began wondering what we would do for work when we got home. How would we afford apartments with no money for a deposit or first month's rent. No one wanted to boomerang home and move back in with their parents. We were all ambitious college graduates with the world at our fingertips … but no one had a job lined up. We had been so busy preparing for the tour and making the demo tape (and praying to God for a record contract) that none of us had thought about, let alone prepared for, a Plan B.

This was particularly disconcerting for my parents. I was the first in our family to graduate with a four-year college degree. My folks were proud of me and had grand plans for my future. They didn't understand and were frustrated by my choice to, from their perspective, become a "wandering minstrel" who was throwing away his hard-earned college degree to go "sing for Jesus and beg for money in churches" rather than pursue a career worthy of his newly minted college credentials. Try as I might, I was unable to explain God's role in my life. So, to my family, I was a failure. When we returned home after the tour, my parents were further dumfounded that I hadn't even thought to prepare for life after Hosanna. They thought I had been particularly remiss and irresponsible given the fact that Lorrie and I had married only five months earlier. The fork in my path loomed very large.

Not coincidentally, when we collected our summer mail being held at the Post Office, there in the pile were three letters from the record companies. Two of them were in regular-sized envelopes and they contained the standard form rejection letter. You know the kind … thanks for your submittal, enjoyed your songs, but not interested. Well, we had asked God to give us definitive direction regarding the future of the band, and those two letters were certainly definitive. But the third letter was different. It was in a larger envelope and contained materials other than just a letter. Could this be the hoped-for direction that Hosanna would make a record and continue touring together?

The letter said the company was interested in the songs, but not the band. They wanted my music but not us as a group. At first this seemed like good news for Lorrie and me. I hadn't really thought about becoming just a songwriter but the idea struck me as interesting. But then, as we read and re-read and prayed over the letter, we began to realize that it was not the answer we had asked for. We had prayed specifically that God would call the band to continue together, not that one of us would be singled out for a songwriting contract. If I had been Gideon, it would have been like God raining on just a portion of the woolen fleece. We had prayed for a specific answer, and as tempting as the alternative presented in the letter was, the answer was no.

When we shared this with our bandmates they were disappointed for the group but, at the same time, they encouraged me to pursue the songwriting opportunity anyway. That was kind of them, but Lorrie and I felt differently. We did not have a peace about changing the terms of our deal with God in the middle of the stream, so to speak. No, we felt it important to remain true to the intent of our original prayer, even though it meant walking away from a potentially attractive career path. We didn't want to manipulate God's answer or play games with the beginning of our life together. We wanted to be obedient and respond with integrity, so we declined the songwriting offer. We had no idea what to do next, but we were convinced that God would provide for us; that God would direct us; and that God would honor our commitment to be obedient to what we understood His decision about a career in music to be. God closed a path we had sought to travel down so we would wait until He showed us another.

One of the last concerts of that summer was a youth retreat at a camp on the Boulder River in south central Montana. The speaker talked about trusting God and giving to Him unreservedly, and then watching for His loving and abundant response. We saw this response in action in a few smallish ways that summer: putting all our gas money in an offering plate and then being blessed with a free tankful of gas at a local service station; foregoing the purchase of new shoes for Lorrie only to be given a perfect-fitting, slightly used pair a week later; and being treated to free access to a drive-in movie by a friend. As our path veered away from music, although disappointed (and even tempted to justify a different choice), we were not disillusioned. We were glad for the direction we received, and we never seriously looked back. Hand-in-hand we gladly took the path less known to us … but well known to God. We were wholly ready and willing to give our lives unreservedly to God and wait for His loving and abundant response. Little did we know that this fork in the road would eventually lead us to another one, with an even more dramatic outcome.

After the direction regarding Hosanna, Lorrie and I set about trying to find employment that would enable us to rent a small apartment and buy groceries. We stayed with Lorrie's folks for two weeks while we prayed and investigated job possibilities. One such possibility was with a former employer of mine who was now managing a thriving, five-star hotel in Seattle. I had worked my way through college in the hotel business, and so I knew quite a bit about it. Seattle seemed a long way from Montana, and our heart was to stay in the state I had grown to love. But with no other real prospects and feeling our welcome at the Marks' home was waning (which, of course, it wasn't ... it was more me itching to get out and establish our own independent household), we decided we were going to move to Seattle.

Sadly, resigned to this choice, Lorrie and I drove down to our beloved college town of Bozeman to pick up our things and say goodbye to friends. While there, sleeping on the floor of a good friend's apartment, the thought occurred to me that I should at least make a few calls in town to see if there might be any job opportunities. I'm not sure why I hadn't thought about that before. Perhaps, because all I knew of Bozeman was the college, the thought of actually settling there never crossed my mind. But the more I mused on it the more I became enamored with the idea. We could stay in my adopted hometown and stay in direct contact with our many friends in town. It would be like college without the burden of classes and exams. It would be perfect!

I was surprised to learn of two different but similar job openings. Both jobs involved media-marketing (a.k.a. sales). One was for the local newspaper and the other was for a new radio station with an FM country music format. The radio station was the brainchild of the owner of the most successful AM pop-rock format radio station in Montana. Because the radio gig seemed more exciting, I interviewed there first and was offered a sales position the next day. Everything happened so fast, my head was spinning. Just three days earlier I was planning to pack everything into a U-Haul and drive to Seattle, but instead I was now looking for an apartment in Bozeman. God was indeed good. It was a blessing we had literally never even thought to pray for.

Since our few belongings were already stored in a friend's garage in Bozeman the move was fairly simple. Our possessions at the time consisted of a water-bed, an old rocking chair I had re-finished, a desk, a small bookshelf made of plywood and cinder blocks, some wedding gifts, an odd array of casserole dishes, and … my stump. The stump was my universal and most prized piece of furniture. I bought it at a lumber yard for a dollar during my freshman year in college. It was about two feet tall and had a circumference of about 20 inches. I varnished it to prevent any bugs inside from escaping and nailed a piece of old orange shag carpet on top. It served as my chair, coffee table, card table, footstool and best conversation piece. I treasured my stump, but Lorrie never shared my affinity for the thing. Interestingly, my daughter tells me that such rare furniture pieces are now sold for hundreds of dollars at Anthropology. I guess I was just a man ahead of his time.

Within a week we landed a small apartment on the west side of town. Never was a young married couple happier. I started my radio sales job and Lorrie got a job as a cosmetologist at one of the nicer salons in the downtown. Seemingly overnight we had two incomes (modest though they were), an apartment, plenty of groceries and a new life together. That fall I went hunting and bagged a deer that provided us venison for the winter months. We began buying used furniture at garage sales and at the Goodwill store. We became seriously expert second-hand shoppers. We bought a small, used, round dining table with four captain's chairs for $69. I bought a used orange 10-speed Sears brand bike for $79 (the exact amount the seller needed to cover his rent that month). We even bought a car. It was a silver Honda Civic two-door with front-wheel drive that made my trek out to the radio station, five miles south of town, reasonably safe in the winter snow. Lorrie continued to drive the little 1967 Datsun she'd had from high school (which was literally held together in places by duct tape and Band-Aids). We were able to host dinners for our friends, many of whom were still in college. We started paying down Lorrie's school loans. We had ample room to host the home fellowship Bible study we had started while in college. Our church family warmly welcomed us back from our music tour, and we were able to lead worship occasionally on Sunday mornings. Life was good.

During that first year of marriage Lorrie and I thrived. We met new friends and stayed in touch with old ones. We fell into a comfortable pattern as we adjusted from student life to the work-a-day world of "adult" life. I even coached a Little League baseball team with a friend. The parents all thought it odd that two young 20-something, newly married guys without children of their own would be willing to invest time into coaching, but we did so for the fun of it. Our team was much like the movie, "The Bad News Bears". We had all the classic characters on the team. The "too-cool-for-school" shortstop with gold chain necklace and bright white cleats, the giant (for his age) lumbering "gee shucks" first baseman, the tiny kid who could barely hold the bat level at the plate, and the young one who spent most of his time in right field picking dandelions out of the grass. I still have an old baseball sitting on a shelf that was signed by each of the team members and given to me at the end of the season. I guess I was unknowingly preparing for my many future years of coaching my own kids.

About nine months into the radio job, I began to realize that selling radio ads was not really my thing. Oh, I did well enough at the job (I was actually the top salesperson in the office), but it was hard, grinding work. Selling "air time" for a new station that had no track record (no Arbitron numbers), that played country music on the FM band (farmers didn't have FM on their tractors), at exorbitant prices set by the wildly successful sister AM station, was a tough road to hoe. I spent many long hours in the studio (after my full day of sales calls) producing "demo spots" to try to convince businesses to at least try our station.

I found myself seldom listening to music on the radio. Instead, I was constantly turning to random stations listening to commercials, seeking inspiration for new ideas and trying to find out where my clients were spending their advertising dollars. I became obsessed with the competition of it all to the point of pouring over the newspaper each morning in search of announcements of new businesses in town so I could be the first on their doorstep to pitch radio advertising. This was not a career path I wanted to pursue for any length of time.

I was disillusioned. I had naively thought that my first job would be my forever job. Not true ... and in the late spring I was offered and accepted a different job. I became the operations manager for a start-up company that built, owned and operated a small chain of motels called Thrifty Scot (kind of the Midwest version of Super 8). The parent company was headquartered in Minneapolis, and the son of the founder/owner had decided to live in Bozeman and bring the chain out West. He spent most of his time finding properties and building the motels, and he needed me to help him run the day-to-day operations. I was well-suited for the role given my background, so I left the radio station and stepped back into the hospitality world. A modest pay raise and a company car accompanied the transition. Finally, I thought, a career opportunity I can really embrace and plan our future around.

I went back to Minnesota for a week of "corporate" training and met the home office crew. While there I got the sense there might be some degree of discomfort with the "son" launching his own management company, but I figured it was just internal family politics. While in Minnesota I met up one evening with an old musician friend of mine. He had taught me some of the finer points of playing guitar during my freshman year and we were both Dan Fogelberg fans. Unlike my current "business world" path, he was in full pursuit of his musical career dreams. He was singing at night in various clubs and bars and seemed totally in love with the lifestyle. Of course, I wouldn't have been singing in bars, but still, seeing him reminded me of my not-too-long-ago dream and I was surprised by the fact that, and my disappointment from the closure of our music path still seemed fresh. But I reminded myself, although I might not understand it, being in God's will regarding direction and path would always be the "right" place for me in the long run, despite my emotion driven pining's to the contrary.

When I returned to Bozeman, I settled into my new responsibilities. The company was quite small, in its infancy really, with only four properties to manage. I quickly mastered the day-to-day routine and looked forward to developing systems and programs as the management company grew. Lorrie and I felt like we had finally found "the" path God had for us. This felt much more like a career than the radio job. But just as things were hitting a smooth pace, the bottom dropped out unexpectedly.

My boss's father and his Minnesota corporate minions decided it would be best for the parent company to unify all property management under a single umbrella. In other words, father told son, if you want to build and own Thrifty Scot motels, you'll need to do it my way. Of course, what could the son do other than obey his father. So, in the span of time occupied by a single phone call, my job, my anticipated future, and my new career path were all effectively eliminated. My boss felt terrible knowing I'd left the radio station to join ranks with him, so he offered me the opportunity to manage one of his motels in Casper, Wyoming. We flew down to Casper in his private jet to see the property. It was nice enough, but I just couldn't see myself as a live-in motel manager in the middle of dusty Wyoming. No, that alternative was not a path I wanted to explore. So, I was "laid off".

I must say that being unemployed, in the official sense, was a very humbling experience. In order to make rent and cover the most basic expenses, I was forced to apply for state unemployment benefits. Being a fairly staunch conservative, pull-your-own-weight kind of guy, I was extremely distressed to have to ask for and receive a government handout. I know it wasn't untoward or abusive of the system for me to do so, but it just didn't sit well with me. Nevertheless, for the sake of keeping us afloat, I humbled myself and opted into the system.

During this period, I became recommitted to finding "the" career path for our life. I spent a great deal of time in prayer and sought after many local jobs. None were, however, anything more than just stopgap measures. Fortunately, I was able to find interim employment for nine months at Montana State

University, where I had graduated a little over a year earlier. I was hired as an "assistant instructor" in the Business School's Marketing Department. I was basically a glorified teacher's assistant. I ran marketing lab classes and tutored students. Not a bad job really. It was pretty much a nine-to-five gig with lunches at the tennis court with a buddy of mine. So I was able to get off the government dole, but I knew the job was only temporary.

After I got the university position, Lorrie and I talked about setting out another fleece, this time for a long term career path. God had been very faithful in answering our last trek into this faith arena, and we had no reason to expect He would not be so again. But, I was hesitant because the last time God's answer was not what I had selfishly wanted it to be, and I knew if I asked for Divine direction, I would again have to be obedient to the response.

I wanted more than anything else to stay in Montana. We were willing to leave Bozeman if necessary, but we had to stay in-state … after all, that's where our families were. So, I sheepishly decided to hedge my bets. I can confess this to you here because God knew full well what I was doing. You can't fool God, no matter how clever you think you might be. My hedge was to pray specifically (i.e., set out the fleece), but give God lots of time to answer (translated: so I would have plenty of time to find a career job in Montana on my own). So, in June we asked God to give us specific direction by the end of the year. This time I didn't ask, or even suggest, what form the direction would come in because I wanted to leave all "my" options open. I imagine God was saddened (or maybe humored) by my faithlessness in pursuing Him this way. I really wanted to trust in His direction and provision. He had proven Himself in the past. I really needed His help. Yet, I just couldn't completely release the process. At the time of our Hosanna prayer, I had not yet experienced any life of personal responsibility, so maybe I had become deluded about my own abilities due to the modicum of success I had achieved? (Again, a laugher for God, I'm sure.)

During the ensuing months, while working my instructor job, I spent many hours pursuing everything imaginable in Montana. There were countless letters and resumes and interviews. I even received several job offers, but all of them struck me as resulting from my efforts rather than God's direction. It seemed I was in direct conflict with myself. I had set up the "hedge" in my prayer so I could control the outcome but then couldn't bring myself to take advantage of it. I guess deep in my soul, I really wanted to trust God and follow His direction for our future. I just had to get myself out of the way.

Among the scores of things I pursued that summer came an odd invitation. While playing tennis I casually asked a friend what he was planning to do over the weekend. He told me he had been studying for months for an exam he was going to take that weekend. He was very excited about it. It was called the LSAT- the Law School Admission Test. He said it only cost $50 to sign up and that if I had nothing better to do I should join him in taking the exam. I hesitated as I thought: what? ... go back to school? ... for three long years? ... "law" school? ... hadn't he seen the movie "Paper Chase"? Didn't he know the pain and suffering he would be signing up for if he passed the test? Was he crazy? Was I crazy? Well, as random as it seemed at the time, I paid the $50 and sat for the exam. No studying, no prep (other than to preview the "types" of questions that might be asked) and, as a result, really no anxiety about the whole ordeal. My friend and I joked about it afterward and, a few weeks later, it was all but forgotten.

As the end of the year approached, I began getting anxious about the impending answer to our fleece that I knew was coming. I was curious how, exactly, God might choose to speak to me this time since I hadn't pre-requested any particular form of response. Maybe I should have? My mind wandered as I imagined all kinds of communications, but all I could be certain of was that something extraordinary was going to happen soon and we had to be on the lookout for it. As the year-end grew closer, Lorrie and I would quiz each other each evening as to whether we had experienced anything unusual that day that "might" be an indicator of direction. We knew the Bible recorded many different (and some even bizarre) manifestations of God speaking to His people so in our mind nothing could be considered off the table.

The end of the year, December 31, finally arrived. I remember the sense of adrenaline I had that morning as we kissed each other goodbye and promised to rendezvous back at the apartment for a peanut butter and jelly luncheon. I reminded Lorrie that "something" big was going to happen that day. The morning passed uneventfully. While enjoying lunch at our little $69-dollar table scrunched into our kitchen the ordinary suddenly became the extraordinary.

The mailman arrived to make his usual noon delivery and seeing us through the window, he walked up to say hello and hand-deliver the mail. After we exchanged pleasantries for a moment the carrier left and Lorrie and I sat back down to finish lunch. Leafing through the day's mail, I saw an envelope that made my heart skip a beat. It was a formal-looking piece of correspondence with the acronym "LSAT" noted in the return address space. Uh...LSAT...wasn't that the test I had taken in the summer? Yes, that was it, the law school test. Oh no, not law school, Lord. Three years of "Paper Chase?" My mind began racing. "Go on," Lorrie implored, "open it!"

This was the extraordinary communication we had prayed and waited for. This was how God had chosen to answer our fleece. Even before

I cracked the seal, I knew this meant I must have passed the exam. I knew this meant going back to school. I knew this meant leaving the comfortable life we had carved out (albeit tenuously) and heading into a very great unknown. Like Moses being sent back to Egypt. Like Joshua being sent to Jericho. Like Paul being blinded on the road to Damascus. I knew I had no choice but to read the letter and obey God's direction.

The letter made several aspects of the direction clear. We were going to law school. Not only had I passed the exam but I also scored in the 99th percentile, in other words one of the highest scores in the country. This was exciting, of course, but also frightening in that we realized the score, combined with my college G.P.A., likely meant we would be leaving Montana. You see, the only law school in Montana didn't require a very high score to gain admittance, and I learned later that the only other person in Montana to score above the 90th percentile was going to go to the University of Montana law school because her husband and family lived in Missoula. Of course, that didn't preclude me from also going to U of M, but it did mean I had a very good shot at going to one of the more prestigious schools in the country. I had been told all the big schools like to have at least one student from each state and given my score I was the odds on favorite to represent Montana. I also had the distinct sense that in answering us in this dramatic way God had some bigger plan for us than I could have ever imagined. As we ventured down this new path in prayer, we became more and more convinced of that. This was, indeed, going to be a tectonic shift in direction for us.

Given the seemingly endless opportunity potential of the LSAT score, we decided we should apply to several of the most influential and important schools in the country. We prayerfully considered our options and chose six schools. We could not afford to apply to more than six because the application fees alone were $75-100 per school. Of course, our list included Harvard and Stanford. We also selected top-tier state schools in the West; University of Washington, University of Colorado, University of California at Berkeley, and University of California at Davis.

Since this was not just about "my" life, I wanted to include Lorrie in every step of our decision. We had been counseled by a trusted Christian attorney friend at our church to treat the next three years as if we were divorced and then hope to reconnect when school was over. While that seemed somewhat logical, for purposes of immersing myself in my studies, it didn't sit well with either of us. So, instead we resolved to take each and every step together, hand-in-hand, all the way. Committed to traveling the path together, Lorrie and I separately ranked the six schools we had selected in terms of our personal preference and then we compared lists. Of course, my ranking related to school prestige and national reputation. Lorrie's, on the other hand, related more to location and lifestyle opportunities. When we compared our lists, UC Davis was third on Lorrie's and fourth on mine. We began thinking perhaps that would be a good choice. God then helped us a bit with our decision.

Harvard declined my application (I guess they already had a Montanan in another class). I was actually happy about this rejection because I really didn't want to move to the East coast. Stanford "wait listed" me, meaning if all their first-round invitees didn't accept, I could be offered a slot in the second round. This was very exciting news because most of the big schools would likely have similar first-round candidate lists, and as students choose one school or another there would inevitably be opportunities in the second round. We received acceptance letters from the other four schools, but Davis continued to have a special allure, mostly because of how it had fallen on our personal rankings lists ... in the middle for both of us. Then, Davis began pursuing me with scholarship offers and waiver of out-of-state tuition fees. Maybe it was the wooing, or maybe it was our commitment to walk the path as a couple that we thought God would honor, or maybe it was the fact that I had grown up in the Sacramento area near Davis and had some general familiarity with the community, or maybe it was all of these factors and/or others, but, in the end we chose to attend Davis. So, now I joke I had the distinction of turning Stanford down before they could make me a second-round offer. Yeah right … but it sounds good anyway.

With our path now defined by the patient and loving voice of God, we were able to finally rest after two years of turmoil and uncertainty. Sure, we were anxious about what might lie ahead in three years of "Paper Chase", but we were confident that God would see us through and continue to direct our future together. And then, as if to put icing on the cake, that summer before law school God brought Hosanna back together again and we went out on a second tour. It would be one more music ministry opportunity for us before heading off to lawyer-land. This time we knew it was only a temporary excursion, but we loved it nonetheless.

Our travels with Hosanna (both tours) were filled with spiritual awakening, wonderful fellowship, fruitful ministry, adventure and more than a few laughs. The night before Hosanna left on our first tour we gave a concert in our college town of Bozeman. It was a combination farewell and bon voyage. We performed in the old theatre downtown to an audience of nearly 200 people from the local community. Afterward a small group gathered with us backstage for prayer. It was an emotional time for all of us because having just graduated we realized we might not again see many of these friends we had grown so close to during the preceding four years. The prayer time was long and intense, and as it came to a close one of the leaders from our church was moved to ask God to grant me strength and wisdom as I led the group out to serve that summer.

That word was powerful and significant because the group hadn't really talked about how we would manage ourselves during the trip. We were all friends and peers and in the excitement and busyness of the past year, we never really talked about "leadership". It would, of course, be important that one of us have responsibility for the final say if we came upon an issue about which agreement could not be reached. Perhaps we never discussed it because no one wanted the job. I certainly didn't ... but by that prayer it was squarely placed on my shoulders.

To my surprise (and somewhat to my chagrin) each member of the group agreed with the word that had been spoken imposing this mantle on me. When all were finished praying, there was nothing I could really do other than accept the assignment. Assuming responsibility for the tour was an uncomfortable yoke for me at first, but as the summer unfolded everyone worked well together as a team, and fortunately during our eight-week adventure, very few circumstances arose that required any real exercise of authority. In looking back, I think that may have resulted from the fact we were all following the leading of God's Spirit and the leadership role had been, in essence, Divinely assigned, rather than sought after or contended for, so everyone was content to embrace and follow. I learned much from the role. We all would learn much from our experiences that summer.

We performed in a different town each night. Before each concert the local congregation would often host a pot-luck dinner for us, and we all became quite familiar with many different kinds of potato salad and fried chicken. After each concert service we would be sent off to separate private homes for the evening. I had expected our concerts and music would be how we would bless people, but I quickly learned it was actually in these homes, long after the concerts ended and sometimes late into the evening, that the real ministry would take place. For some reason Lorrie and I were often placed with elderly widows or broken families. Perhaps the pastors thought as newlyweds we could bring fresh hope into these households. While I would like to think we might have done so, the reality was that we received far more than we could ever have given.

On day four of our first tour we stopped in the rural town of Minot, North Dakota. After the evening service at a local church, we were given our housing assignments. All the home-stay hosts were in town except ours so after dropping the others off, Lorrie and I took the van and headed out into the countryside as the sticky-hot summer sun began to set. We were invited to stay with an elderly widow named Miss Catherine. She was 87 years old and lived on the homestead farm she and her husband (deceased for 12 years) had settled in 1911. She was the "old Saint" of the church, and we looked forward to meeting her. She had been feeling weak so had not been able to make the drive into town for our concert but told the pastor she really wanted to meet "those nice young people from Montana."

Her farm was about seven miles southeast of town. As is typical in a farming community, the directions we received were based on physical landmarks rather than addresses. We were told to head south on the highway for about two miles and then turn left when we saw the old red barn. Then go another three miles or so and veer right again at the "Y" in the road. Then take the next two lefts you come to and then turn right at the old oak tree and you'll see the place down a ways on the right ... can't miss it. It sounded easy enough. The only problem was it got dark and we couldn't see the red barn (our first landmark), so we were lost almost before we started.

Rural North Dakota is a maze of small country roads that crisscross every mile or so. After 30 minutes of trying to find any of the noted landmarks, we abandoned our quest and drove back to town. By now the church was vacant so we drove around town looking for someone who might be able to redirect us to Miss Catherine's farm. A few blocks away we saw a sheriff's car parked in front of a 7-11 Store. We pulled over and found the officer inside. We told him our story and he, of course, knew Miss Catherine and gave us new "in the dark" directions. To our dismay, the sheriff apparently didn't know the countryside as well as he thought and his directions led us exactly to the "wrong" farm house.

Except for the bare sliver of waxing moon that lit the warm night sky, it was pitch dark out in the farm fields. A single light bulb dangled over the porch of the farm house we had arrived at. As I turned the engine off and started to get out of the van, a ferocious pit bull charged from the porch. I quickly retreated back into the van. A man then came out of the house and the light bulb, which was gently swaying in the breeze, cast an eerie silhouette. In the man's hand was what appeared to be a shotgun. As I rolled down the window to ask if this was Miss Catherine's place, the man cocked the big gun. In a gruff and angry voice he accused us of trespassing and ordered us off his property. As he lowered the gun barrel in our direction, I decided this must not be Miss Catherine's farm because she would be expecting us. I threw the van into reverse and high-tailed it out of there! We went back to town and got directions again, this time from a gas station attendant who also happened to be the retired rural postman. He knew the area like the back of his hand and the third time was a charm for us. At just after 11 p.m. we finally pulled in to Miss Catherine's homestead.

Our lovely hostess greeted us warmly with no apparent concern for the lateness of the hour. I suspected she didn't get a lot of company. Though we were exhausted, we graciously received the tea and cookies she had prepared for us. We listened intently as she told her stories while showing us scores of old black and white photos that adorned the walls, the mantle and the top of a well-used black baby grand piano. After an hour of reminiscing she led us up a flight of narrow, creaking, wooden stairs to an attic room she called the honeymoon suite. She told us her husband had built the house for her and that they had honeymooned in this little suite. Her eyes drifted upward and a warm smile graced her face as she told us that she maintained the room in that original condition. The space was dimly lit with candles she had set out especially for us and a beautiful handmade quilt lay on top of the bed. The room was drenched in warmth and love. As we settled in, however, we began to laugh because even the tiniest movement caused the old bed springs to squeak loud enough to wake the neighbors. Miss Catherine glowed as she continued to bless us with her stories during breakfast the next morning. We left that homestead farm house with hope that our romance might be as wonderful and fondly recalled 50 years later.

One Saturday night we sang in a park near Glendive, Montana. The crowd came and went over the course of our 90-minute program, and as we broke down the equipment the sun was setting. One of the unique aspects of our ministry, which we highlighted on our posters, was that we performed some of our songs in sign language. Consequently, now and then we would have a deaf person in the audience. That evening, as we were packing up, a deaf teenager approached Lorrie to have a conversation. As the sky grew darker he had to get closer and closer to Lorrie to be able to read her sign language. Before long they were only a few inches apart. It was an interesting lesson in personal space. Meanwhile, I had been drawn into a conversation with another young man. As we chatted the fellow's voice turned somber as he began telling me about his recent attempt to commit suicide. I was totally unprepared for this and felt way in over my head. Having no skills with which to counsel in this situation, I resorted to prayer. As we prayed together his mood lightened, and when we finished, he seemed relieved and was smiling. After that evening's experiences we all agreed to be more diligent about praying for wisdom and discernment before every service. We were fast learning that ministry is serious business and that our music was merely a vehicle of invitation.

It seemed that every venue presented a unique set of circumstances. In one small town in Idaho, a pastor spoke to us about the negative influence of drums played in church. He had obviously not seen our set-up on the stage in the church sanctuary. As soon as the meal was finished we quickly huddled to discuss what to do about our drum set on the stage. We concluded we didn't have time to remove it as people were already arriving, so we decided we would just have to endure the pastor's wrath later. We prayed for grace. As the concert began the pastor entered the room and sat down in the front row. He bore a cross expression on his face and was clearly displeased to see the drums. The audience response to our music, however, was robust and positive, and by the fourth song in the opening set we were surprised to see the pastor join the congregation in clapping hands to the beat. And he was "smiling"! That night several people came forward during the alter call to accept Christ. The pastor joined us in praying with those folks and together we wept tears of joy, drums notwithstanding.

We also came to appreciate that the denomination name on the church door didn't necessarily define what might happen inside. We played at one Presbyterian Church where the pastor invited us into his office for a pre-service prayer after the usual pot-luck. As we sat together in a small circle the pastor's voice began to quiver. He thanked us profusely for being there and asked us to "please pull out all the stops and melt the congregation down." He then went on to share that although he had been pastoring at the church for 12 years, he had only been a born-again Christian for the past seven years. He expressed disappointment at his lack of success trying to communicate to his congregants the difference between "religious" attendance at church and a "relationship" with Jesus. He was hoping our message might help him share the real truth of the gospel. We were blessed by this servant's candor and his heart for the people.

Because we usually stayed in different homes, when we regrouped in the van each morning to head off to our next destination, we would always compare our home-stay experiences from the previous night. In southern Idaho we were met with a heat wave. That evening

Lorrie and I were assigned to a home-stay host who had to work late and would be leaving early the next morning so we were given directions and a key. When we arrived at the tiny ramshackle house, a note on the kitchen table informed us the air conditioner was broken and instructed us to sleep downstairs in the basement, "where it would be cooler." There was no ventilation in the basement, and it was stifling hot. The pull-out couch bed had a single cover-sheet, and the mattress had a rubber pad on it. That was it. The two old pillows were flat as pancakes. The heat made us sweat, which made the rubber pad stick to us. It was a miserable night of sleep, to put it mildly. When we went back upstairs the next morning our host was already gone. For breakfast he left us two granola bars. As we compared experiences that morning, our drummer, Dave, shared about his evening which had been vastly different than ours. He had been hosted by a wealthy couple. He stayed in a master bedroom suite and slept on a king-size bed with satin sheets and bathed in a Jacuzzi tub in the adjoining bathroom. He was served a three-course breakfast including an omelet, fresh pastry, and fruit. We laughed about the contrast in experiences. Dave's experience

41

gave Lorrie and I hope our next one might be better.

A week later we were hosted by an elderly widower in a small trailer home. The trailer was airy and tidy and the fellow's fastidiousness reminded me of Felix from the television show, "The Odd Couple". The pull-out couch bed was reasonably comfortable though it sagged a bit in the middle. The challenge to this place was the clock on the wall ... actually all the clocks. Nearly every square inch of wall space surrounding our couch-bed in the living room was covered with cuckoo clocks. The man had a collection of more than 50 of them. They were fascinating to look at but they became a problem every 15 minutes. Because they were not synchronized we were regaled with 50 gongs, cuckoos, bells, tweets and whistles over a several minute period. It was far worse at 10, 11, and 12 o'clock, when the top of the hour clamor was almost deafening.

At one week-long youth camp we ministered at, Lorrie and I were offered a small cabin to stay in rather than a tent. Lorrie was thrilled at the thought of a bed for the week rather than a sleeping bag on the ground, especially because rain was in the forecast. After moving our suitcases into the cabin I invited Lorrie in for a look around. When she sat on the bed we heard a small squeak. I thought it was the bed springs, but it wasn't. Several mice ran out from under the bed and scampered across the floor. Lorrie jumped up on the bed in less than a nanosecond and emitted a scream that could be heard throughout the entire camp. Though it rained that whole week, Lorrie was never so happy to lie on the ground every night huddled in a damp sleeping bag in a rain-soaked tent.

Perhaps one of our more memorable experiences involved meeting an angel in the middle-of-nowhere, Utah, at 6 a.m. (on our way to a church in Las Vegas). We left our home-stay accommodations in Provo, Utah, before sunrise in order to beat the heat of the day. About an hour down the road we blew a tire on our equipment trailer. We wobbled to a safe stop, but were all quite rattled. While the girls stayed in the van to pray, the guys stepped out to survey the situation. The tire was in shreds but we had a spare. The problem, however, was that the only jack we had was a bumper style jack for the van. The trailer didn't have a bumper so we needed a different kind of jack. We walked back to tell the girls we would be in for a long wait. We were going to have to hitch a ride to a service station and call for a tow truck. Due to the early hour, we hadn't seen another car for quite a while ... so much for beating the heat.

The girls were totally at peace with this news. "Don't worry boys, we've been praying." Less than a minute later, before we could even get our hitching thumbs out, an old clunker pickup slowed and rumbled to a dusty, coughing stop behind our wounded trailer. An octogenarian farmer, complete with straw hat and a pronounced left-leaning arthritic hitch in his gait sauntered up and matter-of-factly said in a gravelly voice, "You boys look like you could use a hand." Then he smiled a crooked grin as the sunrise peaked over the easterly mountains in the distance. After we explained our plight and without uttering more than a handful of words, the old farmer walked back to his pick-up, retrieved a hydraulic jack (the kind that does not require a bumper), and proceeded to change our trailer tire with the skill of an Indy 500 pit crew chief.

When he finished, he wiped his greasy hands on his overalls, smiled that grin again, waved and walked back toward his truck. We just kind of stood there, hands in our pockets, marveling at the whole scene. When I finally snapped out of my stupor I yelled to the old farmer, "Thank you! Thank you!" His door creaked loudly in the still morning air as he climbed up into his cab and turned to wave to us, "My pleasure," he uttered, "and by the way, my name's Jack." We were too stunned to do anything other than just stand there, mouths agape, and watch "Jack" drive away.

And wouldn't you know it, a few weeks later we had another flat tire as we drove past UC Davis on our way to a church event in Marysville, California. We snacked on ice cream in the 100-plus degree heat while sitting on the curb waiting for the tire to be fixed at the only repair shop we could find open on a Sunday afternoon. We later learned we were sitting just around the corner from where, in a few short weeks, we would rent an apartment during the first semester of law school.

CHAPTER 2 - THE PAPER CHASE

I was rudely awakened by the loud grind and whoosh-release of an 18-wheeler's diesel brake. After a sleep-deprived night in a 95-degree sauna (a.k.a. our camping tent which was pitched at the edge of a busy truck stop near the southern Idaho border), we got under way for day two of our trek to California and law school. It was beastly hot. The speed governor on the U-Haul wouldn't let the rig go any faster than 45 miles per hour as we headed west, up and over Battle Ridge Mountain in the Nevada desert. The old truck whined as it plodded slowly and painfully up the mountain. I almost thought I heard it coaxing itself … "I think I can, I think I can …." The fuel gauge bounced all over the place but the engine temperature gauge was constant. It was buried at "HOT". As we crested the summit I put the truck in neutral and let it coast for a while, hoping the engine would cool down but it never did. Fortunately we had just enough momentum and engine left to limp into the mid-desert town of Winnemucca. The town name, though technically in recognition of the ancient Indian Chief, One Moccasin, also seemed to double as a clever gambling enticement. Whatever the purpose of the name, it was not where I, nor any sane person, would choose to break down on a Sunday afternoon under a sweltering 110-degree sun.

The small town had plenty of tourist-trap motels and a cluster of slot machines at every corner (and in every gas station for that matter), but do you think it would have a park with a shade tree? Think again. Miraculously we found the name and number of the local U-Haul outfit and were able to reach the mechanic on duty (who happened to be at home savoring a Popsicle while watching a ball game on TV and sitting in front of the air conditioner with his wife and kids). While he spent three hours studying the old broken-down engine carcass under the dented hood of our transport, we found "one" tree in the middle of a parched lawn at City Hall, a building easily mistaken for just another corner casino. We sat under that lone tree and sipped disgustingly sweet canned lemonade. Thus was the rather inauspicious start to our law school adventure. Yep, it was shaping up to be a desert experience all right.

We had stuffed all our worldly belongings, as well as those of two friends who also happened to be moving to California, into that old U-Haul truck just two days earlier. We also brought with us our Honda Civic and a beloved friend named Kerri who had generously offered to help us with the move. Kerri took turns between riding with Lorrie in the Honda and me in the U-Haul, switching off every tank of gas or so. Consequently, I had lots of alone time on that long three-day journey. Since the radio didn't work in the truck, all I had to keep me alert were the memories of what had brought me to this point. As we rumbled down the road my mind began to wander to memories of another trip I had made seven years earlier on this exact same highway ... only going in the opposite direction.

As I was growing up, my dad worked for the finance division of General Motors. It was a good job, but in order for him to realize the benefits of promotion we were required to relocate frequently. When I was nine years old, we moved to Rancho Cordova, California, a then-bustling suburb about six miles east of Sacramento. As good fortune would have it, when my dad came up for his next several promotions the Sacramento office was expanding, which enabled him to be promoted in place several times. We ended up living in

Rancho for seven years, from my fourth grade year through the beginning of my senior year in high school. Those are important formative years in the life of a young man struggling to get past boyhood and through adolescence.

In 1973, when I was 14 years old, a neighbor lady invited me to church one Sunday morning. Our family only attended church occasionally and on Easter, but I nevertheless had an interest that harkened back to a kid-oriented Sunday school program I had accidentally tuned into on the television when I was seven. I remember it distinctly because it happened on an Easter Sunday. We didn't go to church that day, but instead went to brunch at a local casino (we lived in Reno, Nevada, at the time) to see a circus show with live elephants. The elephants were impressive as they lifted beautiful girls with their trunks and carefully sat on their trainers without crushing them. As impressive as the behemoth pachyderms were, they were not nearly as impressive as the impact that television show had on me. It didn't fully register at the time, but I was deeply moved by the story of Jesus voluntarily going to the cross to pay the penalty owed for my sins. Although I didn't perceive any "major" sins in my life as a seven-year-old, somehow I knew my heart wasn't right and that what Jesus did was specifically for me.

So, I accepted the neighbor lady's invitation and accompanied her to her church across town. At the church there was a "youth group" of about a dozen kids my age. Because there were two junior high schools in Rancho Cordova and all these church kids went to the one I didn't attend, I was as new to them as they were to me. For reasons I can't explain, we all hit it off and I became a regular at both Sunday school in the morning, and at the Sunday evening youth group meetings. When the neighbor lady couldn't take me and my parents were too busy, I was so enthused about the group I would ride my bike five miles across town to be there. The church kids soon became close friends, and, of course, there was a pretty girl in the group that I had my eye on. I was a typical teenage boy. One night after a Bible lesson from the book of Matthew, I remember taking the teaching quite literally. The lesson had been about praying privately in your own prayer closet rather than praying publicly to seek the commendation of men. During free time after the lesson, when we would usually run amuck around the church grounds and generally raise a ruckus, I snuck off by myself and went into the church's broom closet and prayed to receive Christ. Yes, I was born again in a broom closet.

At first my conversion to faith came easy primarily because my normal non-church world was on the opposite side of town from my spiritual world. The church group kids didn't go to my school, so I could lead, in effect, two different lives: my spiritual one with my church friends on the east end of town and my secular/sports-focused/school/rowdy one with my neighborhood cronies on the west end. It was a perfect best-of-both-worlds situation, or so I thought. Although our town had two junior high schools, it only had one senior high school. So, beginning in the 10th grade, my two very happy and separate worlds collided. I suddenly became accountable to my church friends and had to walk a fine line between being spiritual and being normal (at least what I perceived as normal at that time, not yet being well acquainted with the gift of grace and the freedom it provides). To put it mildly, I was miserable. So I decided to keep my faith in my back pocket during high school. I was never a "bad" kid, but neither was I a saint. I kind of just played at Christianity when it was convenient or on Sunday (or whenever the girl I was interested in at the time happened to be a Christian). This was not satisfactory to me, God or anyone else really, but it was the choice I made as a foolish high school kid trying desperately to figure life out.

One month into my senior year, the year that was supposed to be the pinnacle of my life to that point, my dad received the promotion of a life time. He was offered a position as a branch manager. The problem for me was that this meant we had to leave Rancho Cordova. The branch office he was offered was in Great Falls, Montana. I literally had to look it up on a map. To my dismay, I discovered I was being hauled away from my life in California to be outcast on some lowly prairie in the middle of Hicksville. I begged and pleaded to be left in the care of someone, anyone, in Rancho so I could finish out my senior year. After all, I argued, I would be off to college in a few months so what harm would there be in allowing me a slightly early exit from the nest. But my parents, in their wisdom, refused. So I packed for the journey to cowboy land where the buffalo roamed and the antelope played.

I owned my own car at the time, a 1966 Chevy Impala Super Sport coupe with air shocks, mag wheels and a custom stereo system. She was a very nice ride if I do say so myself. While my parents and siblings traveled in the family car, I insisted on driving alone and behind them in my own car, in my own sorrow, in my own misery, in my own pain. Life as I had known it was over. I felt like I was being dragged to Siberia. I argued with God a lot during that several-day drive. I yelled at Him. I pleaded with Him. I cried out to Him. Finally, utterly exhausted and defeated, I resigned the battle and surrendered. I laid my burden down and I prayed to Him. God listened and spoke to me while I numbly followed that straight-as-an-arrow white line across the Nevada desert. God spoke in a way I had never before experienced. In my resignation, God lifted the burden of my yoke. I realized that perhaps what I was leaving behind wasn't really that great after all. At least in terms of my spiritual walk, it was far from great. Reasoning that I would only be in Montana for a few months, until I graduated and returned to California for college, I decided I would see what God could do with me if I actually allowed Him to be "Lord" instead of just "Savior" in my life. After all, what did I have to lose? If things didn't go well who would know? Montana would be but a distant memory soon enough.

I was suddenly jolted from my musings about that previous eastbound trek and all that had led up to it when … suddenly … the Honda zipped by me with the windows down and Lorrie and Kerri waving their arms up and down in unison like flying birds. Thus returned to my westbound reality, I sighed and smiled at the journey I had been on since that eastbound trek seven years ago, and how incredibly faithful God had been to honor my decision to seek Him more completely. Even though I got saved in that broom closet, I didn't really experience the depth of my faith until I moved to Montana. And now, headed back from whence I had come, back to California, I was embarking on the next chapter of my life with a confident assurance, the kind of "hope" described by the Apostle Paul.

We didn't have any further vehicle breakdowns until we arrived in Davis. As soon as we pulled into town we headed for a gas station to refuel. As we slowed to a stop at the fuel pump, the engine heaved an audible sigh, emitted a distressing clunk, spewed a cloud of dark smoke, and then died ... again. We temporarily abandoned the terminally ill truck and piled into the Honda, found a hotel for the night, and readied for apartment hunting the next day. We had applied for on-campus married-student housing but were on a waiting list. Not knowing how long the wait might be and realizing we couldn't afford to live in a motel or continue to fork out the daily rental fee on the truck, we decided to seek out an interim apartment to live in for a month or two. Intro Week for "1-L's (first year law students) was scheduled to start in just a few days.

Renting a place in Davis, California, is unique. Because it is a college town landlords have incredible leverage over their poor student tenants. Accordingly, they had all colluded to create the "Davis Model Lease" which, among other onerous provisions, mandated a minimum one-year tenancy ... no exceptions! We knew our wait for campus housing wouldn't be that long so our interim housing options quickly dwindled, and I thought we might be forced to hole-up in some God-forsaken, by the hour, day, or week, flea-bag motel. But, to our rescue, or so we thought, we learned there was one apartment complex in town that had opted not to join the Model

Lease cartel. It was called Americana Arms. Not only did they allow month to month tenancy, they also had a vacancy that we could move into that day. What is the old adage: if it's too good to be true it probably isn't? In our haste, and due to our lack of other viable options, we signed the Americana Arms rental agreement on the spot (not so smart for a would-be lawyer) and made arrangements to transfer our belongings from the dead U-Haul at the gas station to our new "home". Within the hour we began to realize why this apparent miracle apartment had been available.

The access door to the hallway nearest our ground floor unit had a bullet hole in it. We were told the cause was a domestic dispute. Such disputes, we later learned, were not uncommon. One time we witnessed a disgruntled wife attack her husband with a flurry of microscope slides wildly flung from a second story window. The hallway had a very unpleasant odor wafting through it. The dog in the unit next to ours howled and whined as if being abused by some insane tormenter. The carpet in our unit was filthy so we borrowed a vacuum from the landlord's office, but instead of sucking the dirt out of the carpet it spewed untold nastiness from its decrepit bag into the air and all over everything in the apartment. The hastily applied fresh coat of paint in the Playschool-sized kitchen was still tacky to the touch (probably painted the day before), and when we opened the drawers next to the sink, Lorrie noticed some bumpy things in the paint. They were cockroaches. They had been embalmed in a coat of dime store paint. Lorrie started physically backing out of the apartment, but it was too late, we had signed the rental agreement. We would begin our new life in California in a roach hotel.

We had read that Davis prides itself on being the "bicycle capitol of the world" and true to the reputation there are more bikes registered in Davis than cars. I still had my orange Sears 10-speed and Lorrie had an old beater bike from college so, due to our severe lack of money we decided we would embrace the Davis mentality and use our car only when absolutely necessary, thus saving on gas and avoiding an expensive campus parking pass. The apartment was less than two miles from campus so the daily round-trip ride would be a breeze, we thought. Well, that fall and winter, we were introduced to El Nino which is a peculiar weather pattern that brings monsoon-type rains for months at a time. For four months, until our wait for campus housing finally came to an end, I don't think we ever completely dried out. We were soaked on the ride to school each morning and then soaked again on the ride home each evening. It was miserable. The only saving grace was that Lorrie got a job managing the law school book store so we were able to ride together each day … and misery, of course, loves company.

I had heard many stories about the horrors of 1-L life. Heck, who hadn't seen the "Paper Chase" movie? Well, to ensure that everyone did in fact see it, the upper classmen hosted a special showing (more like a cruel hazing) at the law school on the next to last night of Intro Week. Popcorn was included. Because there was a short pass/fail "quiz" scheduled for the next day, the final morning of Intro Week, the movie audience decreased in size minute by minute as anxiety about not being ready for our first test grew. One by one, paranoid students, freaked out by the movie, were dropping like flies. I can only imagine that by the end of the movie there were at best, only a handful of students left watching. I don't know for sure because I left about halfway through … to cram.

The actual process of law school was as daunting and onerous as everyone said it would be, times three. Employing the "Socratic method", the professors never actually taught anything. They just asked questions, somehow expecting us to know the answers already. They were purportedly teaching us how to think. But we all adjusted and learned the routine. In fact, we even made a game of it. In home room, an elaborate game of bingo was created based on a seating chart map of students who, when called upon by the all-knowing professor to pontificate on some esoteric legal theory, received a game marker on their seat. About three weeks into the semester a row of seats was finally covered and someone exclaimed "BINGO!" The whole class erupted in laughter … the whole class, that is, except the unknowing prof.

That first semester was the toughest. In addition to being soaked to the bone all day every day (thank you El Nino), I struggled to embrace the fact that the entire semester's grade for each class would be based on a single test at the end. No quizzes along the way to build grade cushion, no extra credit, no projects, no points for attendance … none of the tools I had used so effectively in high school and college to insulate against the possibility of a poor exam performance. The stress of this drove many mad, and we all reacted in different ways. Some became morose and withdrawn. Others compensated through gregarious attempts at rank humor. Still others opted for the more traditional college medications of beer and whiskey. For me, without realizing it, I resorted to food. I had always been a rather fit and thin guy consistently weighing in at about 165 pounds. By the end of that semester, however, I tipped the scales at more than 180. When the stress of exams was over we drove home to Montana for Christmas where I actually "lost" 10 pounds, all the delicious holiday food notwithstanding.

Of course law school wasn't just about studying. Even though the "jealous mistress" occupied the vast majority of my waking hours for three years, Lorrie and I still managed to carve out time away from school for equally important things. I think working those two years before law school gave me an appreciation (or at least an understanding) of a traditional "work" week, in contrast to college life. So, I approached law school much like a job, a 60-plus hour a week job (except during exams when it often exceeded 80). When we finally got into campus housing we were only a short 10-minute walk (or 3-minute bike ride) across Putah Creek, to King Hall where the law school was ensconced. In my second and third years I was assigned a study carrel in the bowels of the law library, which became my "office". I hung an old pale green sheet between the dusty book stacks and my study desk to create a semblance of privacy and I set up shop (coffee pot and all). I left an old tattered pair of leather moccasins in my office and every morning when I arrived to "work" I'd take off my shoes and slip into my moccasins for the day, never leaving the building for the next 12 hours. Monday through Friday, 7 a.m. to 7 p.m. was my norm. When you focus, it's amazing what you can accomplish in 60 hours per week.

This schedule enabled Lorrie and I to establish a life together outside of school. Perhaps most important was to try to protect our time together spiritually. We plugged into a local church and volunteered to help with music. We quickly found ourselves serving as the regular worship leaders, a position we were very comfortable with and thrilled to serve in.

We also formed a successor group to our college days' home Bible study. Each week we would gather together with four other grad student couples for study and fellowship. Some of those relationships sustained us long beyond law school, and life time friendships were formed. As previously mentioned, we had been counseled by a wise sage that we should consider ourselves "divorced" for three years, during law school and then hope to pick up the pieces afterward. We rejected that counsel. We were joined at the hip during our three law school years and our marriage grew strong and healthy as did our walk with Christ. Due to her bookstore job Lorrie actually knew most of the law school students and faculty better than I did. She also took a keen interest in some of my classes. While she didn't care much about the vagaries of civil procedure or corporate taxation, she paid very close attention to my stories about California marital property law (ha-ha).

We also made time for fun. Because we were living way below the poverty line during those years, our fun had to be home-made. We played softball. We rode our bikes "everywhere". We played parlor games and cards with friends (sadly, a lost art to most of today's generation). And, we played Frisbee golf; oh ... did we play Frisbee golf. We created our own 18-hole course running through the UC Davis campus. It started and ended at the front steps of the University Administration building called Mrak Hall, and thus was born the Mrak Muni Golf Course. When we returned to Davis many years after graduation to visit friends, for old time's sake we went to play the course and saw dozens of other students doing the same. I'm told our course remains popular today, 30-plus years later.

When we finally moved into our campus housing unit, at the beginning of my second semester as a 1-L, we were ecstatic. Escaping from the accursed Americana Arms had become one of our most fervent desires. The move was quick and easy, but we decided to abandon our cleaning deposit when, upon moving our bed, we discovered on the wall a thick layer of furry dark green mold in the exact shape of the headboard. Lorrie had never seen mold and didn't know what it was. When I told her she gasped aloud. I think she actually cried tears of joy as we departed.

Our new place in "married-student housing" was incredibly small, but we didn't care. Although very old, the building was reasonably well-maintained. There were no amenities to speak of but there was one oddity ... a 2 by 3 foot hole in the wall, patched with plywood, near the door, at about eye level. We asked around and learned this was where the swamp-cooler was supposed to be installed. Of course that meant we needed to buy one. But, with no uncommitted money in the budget available for such a luxury, we imagined the slow process of melting away in the unbearable summer heat that was soon to be upon us. We were happy to learn used swamp coolers were always coming on the market as students graduated and moved out of campus housing. We were able to purchase a bent and rusty unit for about $100 and it served us well for the next two and a half years. (We sold it after graduation for the same $100.)

Because no one else, it seemed, had any money either we soon found ourselves introduced to a bustling underground bartering economy. Fortunately, we actually had something extremely valuable to barter with; Lorrie's hair cutting expertise. Once word spread of Lorrie's prowess with the scissors, everyone wanted to trade with us. We enjoyed quite a bounty, including canned goods, used books, furniture, clothes, and bike repairs.

Another unique thing we had to get used to was the local train. It passed within 200 feet of our apartment, three times a day. The first time we experienced the rumble of the tracks we thought we were having an earthquake and took cover under our $69 table. The noise and shaking seemed so violent we thought for sure the building would collapse around us, but it didn't. Apparently the old structure had gotten used to the locomotion over the years and the two got along like an old married couple, comforted by the sound of each other's snoring. Eventually we didn't mind the train and, in some strange way, even came to welcome it, as one might the hourly chiming of a clock. We actually took a perverse kind of pleasure in watching our guests react, similar to the way we did, when they were first exposed to the calamity.

In March of my first year we celebrated our third wedding anniversary by going out to dinner at a small restaurant near the Sacramento River. As we looked back at our short married history, we counted our many blessings. Despite the pressures of law school, living under the increasing load of debt attributable to our law school loans, and the occasional pangs of loneliness we felt due to the separation from our families and our beloved Montana, for the most part we were content. So much so that I expressed a degree of concern, during our dessert course, that maybe we were getting too comfortable as a couple. I was beginning to worry that if we followed the typical route and finished school, got a job, paid off our school loans, bought a house, and settled into a community "before" we thought about starting a family, we might not ever have children. So, conventional wisdom notwithstanding, we decided to break the second immutable rule of law school. The first rule was not to be married (we violated that precept long before we entered the hallowed halls of UC Davis); the second rule was never, ever, ever have a baby. As Lorrie and I talked, we both realized we were ready to become a threesome. Thereafter we prayed about it together and felt a confirmation that it was okay with God … so we cast caution to the wind and our little diamond, Noelle Marie, was born the following year, one week before our fourth wedding anniversary.

I landed a fairly good-paying clerkship job the summer after my first year of law school so we were able to save a few dollars in anticipation of our new arrival. We began garage sale shopping for all the baby items we would need. The list was lengthy but we had a blast hunting for ultimate bargains. Doing the math, we calculated that even after the cost of gas we could save a few dollars on many baby essentials by driving to Price Club, a precursor to Costco, in West Sacramento. Over time I think the Honda memorized the route and could take us there on autopilot. The frugality I had observed as a boy (which was necessitated by my father's insistence that my mom remain available at home to raise us kids, and which wisdom we would later employ for our own family), became a highly valued lesson. Because Lorrie and I had both grown up in relatively austere circumstances, simple things were more than satisfactory to us. But I soon discovered that once in a while my frugal notions didn't work so well with the reality of my chosen profession.

In the fall of my third year I began thinking about life after law school. We had always talked about returning to Montana to practice law so I had explored a clerkship with the Montana Supreme Court, thinking that would be a good entree into the legal community there. Things progressed well in that direction, and it began looking like such a clerkship was a very real possibility. But we had also grown close to many friends in Davis, particularly our Bible study group, so the prospect of staying in California also had some appeal. To keep our options open, I decided to enter the recruiting game.

Every week during the months of September and October, law firms from all over the state would descend upon King Hall to interview 3-Ls for possible employment following graduation. To narrow the field, Lorrie and I decided if we were going to stay in California, we would want to live where the quality of life might at least come close to what we had known in Montana. We wanted to find a relatively small town with a grand landscape, outdoor adventure, friendly community and opportunity to carve out a healthy future for our family. To meet these criteria, we focused on three communities in particular: Santa

Barbara, Monterey, and Palo Alto. I interviewed with firms from other areas, but mostly just for the practice it provided. By the time my "big three" came to campus I was ready for them, or so I thought.

An older, wiser classmate of mine, who was in law school as a second career after becoming disenchanted with work as an engineer, took me aside one afternoon following a round of morning interviews. I was, of course, decked out in my best - and only - suit and thought I looked rather dapper. My friend thought otherwise. With caution and kindness in his voice and showing the love of a brother, he put his hand on my shoulder and said, "John, I want you to believe I have your best interest in mind when I tell you this … but you will never land a job offer if you keep interviewing in that suit." I was perplexed and replied by explaining that I saw everyone else wearing pinstripe suits with white shirts and dark ties, just like I was. "Yes," he said, "but have you noticed their pinstripe suits are either black, dark gray, or navy blue." Suddenly it dawned on me what he perceived the problem to be. My pinstripe suit was baby blue, right out of the 70s disco movement. It never occurred to me that what worked at college dances and summer weddings in Montana wasn't exactly the professional look I should be presenting to law firm recruiters. Sheepishly I thanked my friend for his advice and acknowledged the wisdom of it, but I confessed that I only had this one suit and couldn't really afford a new one. He said I couldn't afford not to buy a new one, and then offered to buy one for me if I couldn't do so myself. I was stunned, and humbled. What an amazing display of friendship and grace. That weekend I went to Sacramento and bought a navy blue pinstripe suit. It was definitely not in our budget, and I had no idea how we were going to pay for it. But I realized I was about to enter a world very different from what I knew, and so I'd better start getting used to it.

I received callback interviews (the second step after the on-campus meetings) to firms in all three of our preferred towns. After visiting Palo Alto, I decided it wasn't what we were looking for and so declined the job offer I received there. That left the two beach towns we had zeroed in on. My next callback interview was in Santa Barbara. The firm was very prestigious, and they pulled out all the stops trying to impress us. They flew us down which was a treat because we hadn't been on a plane since our honeymoon. While I met with all the partners in the classic, upscale, dark-paneled, leather-appointed office, Lorrie was entertained for brunch by a select group of partners' spouses, who could have doubled as Stepford Wives. I was driven around town and introduced to the best neighborhoods, "where you could live someday," they said. Our overnight accommodation was a private cottage on the beach, literally on the sand.

Dinner that evening was at the Santa Barbara Yacht Club. We were seated at a round table for 14 that was set with more silverware and glassware than I'd ever seen. The main courses were presented under glass and served with a simultaneous lifting, by seven tuxedo-adorned waiters, of all 14 plate covers and a rousing, "Voilà/Bon Appetite!" The dessert was a dizzying array of bite-size samples of eight different confections. Fine wine and after-dinner drinks flowed (even though we didn't drink them) late into the evening while we were regaled with stories of becoming Santa Barbara royalty, of trial battles won and of shrewd business deals negotiated. I imagined the dinner must have cost more than I had earned during my entire clerkship the summer before. Needless to say we were impressed. Santa Barbara was beautiful, and the next morning, after a spectacular breakfast in bed, Lorrie and I walked hand-in-hand along the beach while the waves lazily lapped at our feet and the gulls cried to the morning sun. We didn't try to break it down or analyze it right then, we just enjoyed the moment and soaked it all in while wondering what in the world we heading into. It all seemed so foreign to us, so not who we were, yet so strangely alluring ... so much like "Turkish Delight" in Narnia.

My next callback was to Monterey. Noelle wasn't feeling well so I made the trip solo. Lorrie and I had talked much about the Santa Barbara experience, even more so after they offered us a position in the firm with a starting salary more than double what I had been earning before law school. The firm, the money, the beach and the whole Santa Barbara royalty thing was seemingly an offer too good to refuse, but neither of us felt a peace about it. Nothing in particular stood out as a problem, but it just seemed pretentious with too much focus on quantity rather than quality of life. No one had talked about their family life, or schools, or church or much of anything outside the law, houses, cars, and the "Club". As I boarded the plane to Monterey, I was hoping for something different.

I was greeted at the airport by a smartly dressed fellow who introduced himself as the firm's "driver". Not a good start, I thought. But instead of the pretentious Santa Barbara-like Lincoln Town Car I was imagining, our ride was a rather inauspicious brown pickup truck. It was down to earth and practical. I liked that. The firm was located near the airport in a new building designed in the classic Monterey-Spanish revival style with a wraparound balcony on the second floor and beautiful landscaping. The sincerity and friendliness of the place hit me like a cool breeze as I was introduced around, not just to the lawyers but to the staff as well. To a person, everyone seemed genuinely happy to be there. The interviews, while very professional and thorough, were less about trying to impress me and more about getting to know me as a person. The partners took time to share personal anecdotes about their families, hunting or fishing. The senior named partner, Lewis Fenton, had an almost magical way about him. I knew instinctively this was a great man. He was at the same time both presidential and grandfatherly. I found myself wanting to just listen to his stories and soak in his essence.

The youngest associate in the office, a fellow named Mark Cameron, took me to lunch down on the fishermen's wharf. No yacht club, no pheasant under glass, no dessert sampler plate, no fancy wine, just a nice lunch, quality conversation, and an honest description of life at the firm and life in Monterey. He took the long way back to the office, along the water. Relatively few words were spoken on the drive back. No sales job was needed. The overwhelming beauty of Monterey Bay spoke volumes to me. Like the siren's call, it sang to me and captured my heart. When I got home that night, Lorrie was lit up with anticipation. She wanted a full report. I just smiled and gave her a deep warm hug. Expecting me to be amped after my big day, she was taken aback by the relaxation and calm she sensed in me. She stepped back and peered questioningly into my eyes for a long moment. In response to her gaze I simply whispered, "I think we're moving to Monterey."

At long last, preparations for graduation commenced. It was a mixed bag of emotions.

On the one hand exultation and relief, on the other hand foreboding and dread. Almost like the "Paper Chase" movie experience during Intro Week where no one stayed through the end of the film, it was hard to relax and enjoy the special occasion when the next day preparations for "the" true final exam of all final exams would begin: the California Bar Exam, passage of which was required to be licensed to practice law. But, we had too much to celebrate to let such distraction rule the day. My folks had flown from Montana to join us. They had long gotten over their disappointment with my initial musical foray into the post-college world and were now exceedingly proud of their first-born. Not only was I a college graduate but a law school graduate - a lawyer in the family. I guess in the world's eyes, and especially in the eyes of my father, a man who grew up in relative poverty on the Outer Banks of North Carolina and who had devoted himself to his children and selflessly and tirelessly worked to help them succeed, a little pride was warranted. For me, however, pride was not on my mind. I was overwhelmed with thanksgiving for having survived the path God had chosen for me, and anticipation for the next life chapter God was about to write through me. My blessings seemed too many to number, principal among them were Lorrie and Noelle.

The ceremony was beautiful and inspiring as my colleagues, many of them friends, each took their turn walking across the stage, donning their Juris Doctor regalia. So much sweat, so many tears, so many hours, so much reading. I had literally given my ability to see clearly at a distance to achieve this prize and was scheduled to get glasses the following week. For me though, I was strangely removed from much of what was happening around me. I was choked with emotion for my family. I thought of little else during the two-hour ceremony. When my name was announced, I took little Noelle from Lorrie's lap, grabbed Lorrie's hand, and the three of us approached the stage. There were some surprised looks in the audience, but no one disagreed with the sentiment. Everyone who knew us understood what was happening. As a family of three, not only were we somewhat of an oddity at the law school, but because of Lorrie's bookstore job, she and Noelle had earned almost celebrity status at King Hall. Two had become one and now we were three, and we would graduate together.

The next eight weeks were the most intense and stress-filled of my life. I was fortunate to have my new employer pay for me to attend the top Bar Review course in the country. I attacked the task with more energy than I had ever devoted to a single goal. I studied 10 to 12 hours per day for eight weeks solid. I only took breaks for church on Sundays, meals, a quick 30 minutes of tennis each afternoon and quality sleep. I got a lot of sleep to protect my stamina and my health. In addition to the outlines provided with the review course materials, I created elaborate outlines of my own that I committed to memory, a process I would compare to memorizing every piece of a complex, three-years-in-the-making, jigsaw puzzle. We had very few outside distractions that summer. Lorrie was an angel, taking care of Noelle and keeping me motivated. Other than coordinating the move to Monterey and planning a post-bar exam trip back to Montana, it was all about the books and nothing but the books. By the time exam week arrived, I was ready.

The three-day exam was held in Sacramento, so I was able to sleep in my own bed each night. It was an all or nothing, pass or fail venture. I had been warned by veterans of the ordeal not to speak with anyone at the end of each test session because of the inevitable tendency to compare thoughts about the questions just answered. Such conversations could be devastating to the psyche and an open invitation for self-doubt to invade and destroy. I was even afraid to answer the phone. So, the evening after exam Day One, Lorrie and I got a baby sitter and went to a movie. I figured that would be a safe place to hide for the evening. But wouldn't you know, about a third my class had the same brilliant idea. We all laughed nervously as we furtively glanced at each other in the theatre lobby. But nary a word was spoken and, true to form with an exam on the horizon, most of the theatre was empty before the final credits began to roll across the screen.

One minor miracle happened in my favor on exam Day Two. One of the two essay questions we were given happened to be on the topic of search and seizure versus individual privacy rights, specifically the constitutionality of drug sniffing dogs in airports. This was a hugely controversial topic in the early 80s. The then-most-recent U.S. Supreme Court decision on the matter was called U.S. v. Place. The miracle was that during my second year of law school, I had argued that very case in an appellate Moot Court competition. Not only did I know the facts, the cited precedents and the holding of the case, I was so intimately familiar with each of the several concurring and dissenting opinions that I could quote various Justices by name. Whatever queasiness I may have felt after exam Day One, I knew I had aced this question and my confidence was buoyed through the remainder of the crucible.

Though we wouldn't learn our fate until Thanksgiving, just having the test behind me was reason to celebrate. But we didn't stick around Davis long enough to do so with my classmates. The next day a moving company (compliments of the law firm) arrived to collect our little apartment's belongings. Everything we owned was loaded into a Bekins moving van except for my infamous stump. Lorrie insisted I leave the stump, which had served me so well for nine years, in a dumpster in the alley. We then piled into our little Honda and left for a three-week road trip to Montana and Canada. I never felt freer than during that trip: just the three of us, a family, on the road to tomorrow.

CHAPTER 3 - MONTEREY

The April before graduation, after I accepted the job offer, Lorrie and I visited Monterey together. The associate who had taken me to lunch during my callback interview was Mark Cameron. His wife shared the same name as mine (only spelled differently, Laurie) and they were married just one week after we were in 1980. We had so much in common that when I returned to Davis after that interview day, I told my Lorrie, "It was almost like having lunch with myself." We became close friends with the Camerons and they were extremely helpful during our first year at the firm. Mark was two years ahead of me in the law practice and more than willing to share his experiences and insights with me. They owned a small condominium in Marina, a town about 30 minutes away. We, of course, had no aspiration of being able to buy a home at that time so they helped us hunt for an apartment. Laurie was particularly helpful, keeping Noelle satisfied in her car seat in the back of the Honda by constantly shoveling Cheerios to her.

We settled on a two-bedroom condo in Monterey. It was only five minutes from the office. Though we had wanted to settle in nearby Pacific Grove, vacancy rates were near zero, and we felt extremely fortunate to find the Monterey condo. In addition to securing a place to live, that April visit was also about introducing Lorrie to some of the other associates at the firm with whom I would soon be working. She didn't really need to get acquainted with the area as we had honeymooned in Monterey just five years before. Who gets to live in the paradise where they honeymooned?

When we got married we were poor college students. We married in Great Falls, Montana, during spring break of my senior year, thinking it would be wise to have a few months together before climbing into the Hosanna van. Our wedding was produced on the thinnest of shoestring budgets because there was simply no money. But we didn't mind, we were young and in love. Lorrie's engagement ring was quite modest, and though my brother joked it came from a gumball machine, it was a real diamond, a quarter-carat marquise-cut that I paid for with tips collected over two summers working as a hotel bellman. Lorrie still wears that ring today. It is a testament to who we were and who we are: a man and woman forever bound together by a timeless, simple, and immutable love.

The day I finally paid off the ring I picked it up from the jeweler after work. I then went directly to Lorrie's house to pick her up for a barbecue planned that evening at my folks' house. Lorrie's dad, Gene, a gruff but loving old soul, was sitting on the front stoop of the house applying Shoe-Goo to patch a hole in his fishing waders. When Lorrie saw me pull up she came skipping out to the car. She was so full of life, so full of love, so beautiful, so perfect! As soon as she got into the car and closed the door I just couldn't help myself. The ring was burning a hole in my pocket, so I just kind of blurted out the proposal, right there in the driveway (so much for romance). The question wasn't really a surprise to Lorrie, although I'm sure the timing and circumstance were. She leaned over with stars in her eyes and kissed me. "Of course I'll marry you, John," she whispered in a romantic voice that caused my heart to skip a beat. "What did my dad say when you asked him?" Oops, in my haste and despite my best intentions (I had actually planned all of this to unfold very differently) I neglected to ask Gene. I sheepishly confessed my faux-pas, hopped out of the car and walked resolutely over to my future father-in-law.

At first he pretended not to notice me as I stood awkwardly before him. He finally peered up over the top of his glasses, "You need something, John? I'm a bit busy here with my boots." Having no speech prepared, I plainly said, "Gene, what would you say if I asked you if I could marry Lorrie?" He looked back down at his boots and squeezed another blob of the magic goo onto the toe of the boot. Without making eye contact again he replied in a dead-pan voice, "Well, what would you say if I said no?" I stumbled back a step and began to stammer. Gene then laughed a warm, fatherly laugh, dropped the boot and the goo and stood to give me a burly hug. "Of course you can! We'd be thrilled!" He then beckoned to Lorrie's mom who was in the house, "Shirley! ... Shirley!! Come out here!!! John's got news!!!!"

In truth, when you marry, you marry both your spouse and her family. This was fine with me because the Marks family was wonderful, even though vastly different than mine. I looked forward to learning from them what it meant to be a real Montanan. The Marks clan was a camping, hunting, hiking and fishing group, in contrast to my family who was more about baseball, golf and tennis. Neither was better than the other, they were both great, just different. Gene took me under his wing and taught me how to hunt and fish.

One morning at the crack of dawn we were out on Holter Lake (Gene's favorite fishing spot along the Missouri River), trolling in Gene's held-together-by-duct-tape boat. It was so cold my fingers were numb and ice was forming on my mustache. Sensing my discomfort with the temperature, Gene kindly asked if I would like a cup of hot coffee. I didn't drink coffee but accepted his offer anyway figuring I could at least use the cup to warm my hands. Gene was already using the top of the thermos as his cup so he rummaged around under the seat of the boat for something to pour coffee into. He finally pulled out an old Styrofoam cup and exclaimed, "Here we are, this'll do!" I recognized the cup - it still had the tell-tale dirt clods in the bottom. It was the cup that had held the night crawlers for bait. Gene gave it a good blow and then dipped it over the side of the boat into the lake water, the lake water that had a rainbow-sheen on top of it from the oil leaking out of the boat engine. "There, all cleaned out for you, John." Gene filled it from the thermos and then watched me expectantly to see how I enjoyed the hot brew. Realizing I had better play along to please my father-in-law-to-be, I took a big gulp and smacked my lips, "um-um," I said. In truth, I think cream and sugar might have been better condiments than the worm remains and Valvoline 10-40 were. My new family was certainly going to be an adventure.

Our low budget wedding was unique and therefore memorable in many ways. We created wedding invitations on a Xerox machine and then tri-folded the papers. Rather than buying envelopes, to make the folded invitations look fancy we bought gold seals, about the size of a quarter, from Woolworths. Sadly, we ended up having to cut the seals into thirds with scissors to save money. Not so fancy after all. Lorrie bought a set of little rubber molds at the dime store that we used to make homemade party-favor mints for the reception. Lorrie's mom Shirley baked little buns, and we sliced luncheon meats and cheeses for mini-snack sandwiches. Ladies from the church made salads, and a friend made a cake for us. Lorrie made little flowers from fabric Gene brought back from his final tour in Vietnam and stuffed birdseed into each bloom to be tossed at us as we exited the church. Our wedding photos were a collection of snapshots our friends and family took during the ceremony. The music was all done by our Hosanna bandmates and we even had a sign language dance performed to one of our favorite songs. It was called, "To the Morning" and was the first song recorded on Dan Fogelberg's first album. The tender melancholy ballad became our anthem during the first year of our budding romance while Lorrie was at home in Great Falls finishing high school, and I was away in Bozeman for my freshman year of college. Oh how long it seemed were the days between postal deliveries of our love letters.

Among the memorable moments from the ceremony was when my best man (who was my brother Andy, age 16) turned white and fainted. It was quite a scene when my dad and two other men leapt over the railing and up onto the stage to haul him to a back room. As he started falling, Lorrie and I were kneeling in prayer. He and I had earlier agreed that he would keep the wedding ring on his finger to ensure he wouldn't lose it. As he began to buckle, I calmly reached up and slipped the ring off his finger. Apparently no one saw me do this because a panic set in in the back room where they practically strip-searched Andy's limp frame looking for the ring. When my dad signaled to the audience that the ring was lost, all the moms in the front row began tugging at their own rings hoping to pass "something" to me to give to Lorrie when the key moment arrived. When I eventually produced the wedding ring from my pocket, an audible sigh of relief rippled through the small chapel. The wedding and reception were all we had dreamed they would be. Our family and friends celebrated us and then sent us off as royalty. Of course we couldn't afford the then-conventional Hawaiian honeymoon either, so we opted instead for Carmel-Monterey.

I had visited Monterey once as a kid on a rare family vacation that did not involve driving to Portland, Oregon, where my grandparents lived and near where I was born, so I knew it was a special place. The day after our wedding, we flew into San Francisco. I'll never forget Lorrie on the plane (her first flight ever) as we approached the SFO airport. She was in the middle seat on the left side of the plane. As the ocean appeared through the window, Lorrie craned her neck practically falling into the lap of the elderly lady in the window seat. "It's green!" she exclaimed to the entire plane full of passengers. "Oh my, dear, have you never seen the bay before?" asked the old lady. Everyone laughed out loud. When we pulled out of the terminal in our tiny rental car, Lorrie pleaded that we go directly to the ocean. I wanted her first view of the Pacific to be memorable so we headed to the Golden Gate Bridge and crossed over. It was absolutely glorious. On the north side of the bridge, we dropped down into the little harbor town of Sausalito. While I was plugging the parking meter, Lorrie took off on a dead run down to the harbor. She knelt and lapped a handful of water. "Yep, it's salty all right!" At that moment I had an inkling she might be a beach girl deep down inside.

We enjoyed three nights at a wonderful B&B in Carmel, just a block from the famous white-sand beach. It was mid-March (and still snowing in Montana), so we were the "only" sun bathers on the entire mile-long stretch of beach. I think we got more wind-burned than sunburned, but it didn't matter. Nothing matters when you are madly in love and on your honeymoon. Even running out of money on day four of our seven-day trip and having to relocate from our quaint Carmel B&B to the Motel 6 in North Monterey didn't matter to us.

So, living where we honeymooned was about to become a reality for us. In every way that Santa Barbara had screamed quantity of life, Monterey calmly communicated quality of life. Our choice of law firms had been easy, and I was excited for Lorrie to meet some of the other wives. A week prior to that April visit, spring had arrived, and the Peninsula sparkled like a freshly polished gem. We had been invited to the home of one of the associates for appetizers before a dinner that had been planned with several members of the firm. I had written the somewhat complicated directions to the associate's house down carefully as I didn't want to be late for the special evening that had been arranged for us.

Soon after leaving our hotel, however, I began second guessing my notes. The directions took us into an exclusive area called the Aquajito -- a small mountain community adjacent to Highway 1 that separates Monterey from Carmel. The mountain was dotted with sprawling houses on large lots surrounded by forest and enjoying unparalleled, panoramic views of either Monterey Bay to the north or the Pacific Ocean to the west. My directional uncertainty was due to the fact we were going to an "associate's" house. I knew the salary offer I received was generous, but I hadn't realized what it might enable us to afford in terms of someday buying a house. This associate had only been with the firm for three years!

With no choice other than to press on, I followed the directions higher and higher up into the Aquajito, and as we climbed the houses kept getting grander and grander. Eventually we came to a single-lane private drive that continued winding even higher. Just shy of the literal top peak of the mountain we arrived at a stately gate with a call box. I pushed the call button on the box, half expecting guard dogs to descend and usher us unceremoniously back down the hill to some place we might belong. To my relief and somewhat to my surprise, the familiar voice I had been expecting boomed through the box, "Welcome! Come on up!"

The massive gate slowly opened, and we proceeded up to the grandest estate on the mountain. It enjoyed a 270-degree unobstructed view of Monterey Bay and the Pacific Ocean. As we approached the entry (a huge wooden door that looked like it might have adorned an old Tuscan church in a previous life), Lorrie and I both displayed an expression of reverential awe. As our new friends gave us a tour of the palatial estate and its room after room of stunning views, I finally gathered my composure enough to make a feeble joke about my surprise to see how well the firm treated its associates. My friend laughed as he called his wife and Lorrie into our conversation. With a grin as big as Texas he exclaimed, "We don't own this place ... we are house sitting for a client who is away in Europe for several months." The ice was not only broken, it completely melted. An instant bonding took place with this couple who would be our friends for the rest of our lives.

We officially arrived in Monterey on the first of September, 1985, but I didn't start work until the first of October. After settling into our little condo, we spent that first month getting our bearings and establishing the necessary local bank, utility and other business relationships. One thing high on my list was to find all the beach access points between Monterey and Big Sur. So, every morning for 30 days Lorrie packed us a picnic lunch and we (my bride, myself and Noelle Marie) would head off in the Honda. With neither map nor directions, we just slowly followed the coast line as close as we could and stopped at every apparent access point. We discovered several hidden gems during this exploration that would eventually become some of our favorite places. One such spot was a secluded stretch of sand between Carmel River Beach and Monastery Beach. Due to a unique outcrop of rocks there, we named the place "Eagle Rock", and we still go there regularly to this day.

About a month after I started work, we heard through the mother of one of the other associates (sometimes it really is about who you know) that a small house she managed for an out-of-town owner would be coming available for rent in mid-November. The home was in Pacific Grove (affectionately known to locals as "PG"), the town we really had our hearts set on settling in. Not only that, but it was located at the water's edge on aptly named Ocean View Boulevard and was only one-half-mile from Lover's Point Park (our favorite beach)! Was it too good to be true? No, this time it was absolutely true. The rent would be more than our little condo but this was "on the water" and in PG. We just couldn't pass it up.

That little house was our first introduction to what we would eventually come to understand is the norm in Pacific Grove, namely, that most houses in PG have some, well, let's just say "unique" characteristics. The house was, as represented, near Lover's Point and faced the water on Ocean View. It was a two-bedroom, two-bath arrangement with a lock-off space on the second floor the owners used when they were in town. The place had been decorated in the early 60s. The bright red shag carpeting was nearly two inches thick. Every wall had large mirrors positioned so that you could see the bay from any direction in the house. The kitchen was small and old and reminded me somewhat of my grandmother's in Portland. The windows were single pane and on a windy night, even with the windows locked shut, the curtains flew around. We bought several portable space heaters and moved them around from room to room to stay warm. I'm not complaining mind you, just reporting. It was actually kind of entertaining in all of its uniqueness and to live on the water's edge in PG I would have gladly lived in a tent, which, by the way, is what preceded the house on this property back in the days when Pacific Grove was a Methodist summer retreat.

A minimum one-year lease was required. I was familiar with that kind of prerequisite due to my dealings with the infamous Davis Model Lease years before. Though I would have signed almost anything to live in this place, I did need to be responsible. It wouldn't be prudent to agree to pay 12 month's rent before knowing if I'd passed the bar exam, or, if I would still have a job if I didn't. So, I offered, and the landlord accepted, a 25-percent rent premium each month until I found out the bar results in return for the option to break the lease if I had to. We couldn't really afford that rent premium, but I figured it would only be for a month or two. So we inked the deal and scheduled to move in on December 1. By this time we had become good friends with many of the other associates, and they all pitched in to help transfer our belongings. Friendship, pizza, and soda are a great combination when moving and we would capitalize on that combo several times in the years to come. After we announced to our friends from Davis where we were living, I don't think we were without weekend guests for a year. Living on the beach is a very popular thing, you know. Historically the bar results came out in late November-early December of each year.

Legend had it that results came in two forms: a large envelope or a small envelope. The small envelope was supposedly the coveted prize because the large envelope was said to contain application materials to retake the exam. Strangely reminiscent of that New Year's Eve lunch date four years earlier in Bozeman, I came home from the office to meet Lorrie and Noelle for a quick bite on the Wednesday before Thanksgiving Day. While we were dining on peanut butter and jelly sandwiches, the mail arrived and with it was an envelope from the State Bar. It was ... medium-sized? I had no idea what that might mean. Had the legend been wrong? No one ever said anything about a medium-sized envelope? As I slowly opened the envelope my future, it seemed, hung in the balance. The last four years of my life were now relegated to a single medium-sized envelope.

My mind calculated the options. Would the firm keep me on as a clerk while a studied for and took the bar exam a second time? Could I muster the strength and resolve it would take to do it again? If I lost the job, would we go back to Montana? Would I have to go back to the radio station? Did farmers have FM radios in their tractors now? How would I pay off the law school loans? How would I reconcile my failure with God's clear direction to us? Where were my old Hosanna bandmates? Would they be interested in going out on a third tour? These and many other questions flew through my consciousness in a matter of seconds, much like the experience I'd heard about when one's life passes before them at the brink of death. I opened the envelope. My mind went blank, my knees weakened, and I sat down, mute. I had passed.

With the bar exam forever behind us and our move to Pacific Grove complete, we were finally able to settle into a semblance of routine. Work was consuming, but we still made time to develop friendships in other arenas. One thing I opted into was a men's slow-pitch softball league. Several guys from the office were on a team, and they invited me to join. The games were fun, and I met several people outside of the law practice. The only problem was that the games were often held late into the evening, at times starting as late as 10 p.m. After long hours at the office, the last thing I wanted to do was drag myself out of the house to start playing softball at about the same time I should have been going to bed.

Most of the games were played at a field in the middle of Monterey near El Estero Lake. It was a classy ball field with outstanding lights and bleachers. Of course, at 10 p.m. the bleachers were always empty (though my girls made an occasional trip to watch me play when we had a 6 p.m. start). One evening while playing centerfield, a strange thing happened in the fourth inning. The sea lions down at the wharf began barking raucously and a spectacularly thick fog bank, reminiscent of an old Sherlock Holmes movie, rolled in and blanketed the field. I could not see the pitcher's mound, let alone home plate from centerfield. It was the first time I experienced a softball game canceled due to fog. Monterey was truly a unique place.

I immensely enjoyed practicing law. As I got to know everyone, my impression of the firm grew more and more favorable. This was truly a wonderful place to work. The welcome I had felt when interviewing never changed, and the lawyers and staff were, to a person, top notch. I think much of the firm's culture was due to the influence of its founder and leader, Lewis Fenton. I first met Lewis during my callback interview and had been extremely impressed with the man and his presence. One afternoon Lorrie stopped by to deliver something to me at the office, and, of course, she had Noelle in tow. When she came upstairs I took a few minutes to introduce my girls around. Lewis happened to be strolling down the hall and chatting with the staff (a practice for which he was beloved) when he spied Noelle out of the corner of his eye. With a deep warm voice that had enchanted many jurors, he said to Noelle, "Well, hello there, and who might you be?" Noelle responded by introducing herself with classic 2-year-old bravado. Lewis was smitten. After greeting Lorrie and me, he asked if he might usher Noelle down to his office for a treat. We consented and off they went hand-in-hand, the great Lewis Fenton and our wee toddler. Several minutes later, we wandered down to relieve Lewis of duty and to our surprise found him sitting cross-legged on the floor with our daughter playing with some toys he had fetched from his credenza. One of the most revered attorneys in California was sitting down on the floor entertaining a two year old. That vision spoke volumes to both Lorrie and me. We were definitely in the right place.

The firm had a somewhat formalized training regimen: six months on the business/transaction side of the practice followed by six months on the litigation side. At the end of the first year, you were supposed to discuss performance and long-term interests with the partners and then choose a permanent practice group. At the end of my first year, I had to honestly say I enjoyed both practice areas so much that I didn't really care where I landed. I offered that I'd gladly serve in whatever group had the greatest need. Well, at that time it so happened that a very specialized area of the firm's practice called Land Use (a practice "group" that consisted of a single partner who later became my professional mentor and to whom I will always be grateful) had a need for assistance. A major development project had just been approved and compliance with hundreds of permit approval conditions had to be handled. Many of those conditions involved the preparation of complex legal agreements as well as additional permitting for tangential projects and construction.

Land Use seemed to me like the perfect blend of the other two practices: the creativity of document preparation and drafting on the one hand and advocating for your client in a public forum on the other. I gladly volunteered to assist with the project, which was a major resort, golf course and exclusive residential enclave called Spanish Bay located on the shoreline of the Del Monte Forest, also known as Pebble Beach. Over the next many months, I grew to enjoy Land Use more than I had either of the other two practice areas I had been introduced to and asked if I might stay on in that niche of law. Fortunately for me, that practice area was expanding and my mentor needed a full-time associate, so I was permanently assigned to the Land Use practice (which thus became a two lawyer "group"). I found myself immersed in the legal aspects of constructing Spanish Bay as well as planning for various other future development projects around the peninsula and up and down the coast. I spent much of my time with technical consultants such as land planners, biologists, foresters, engineers, architects, geologists, hydrologists and myriad other technical professionals. I was exposed to as many non-legal issues as legal, and I reveled in all of it. Among the perks of the practice was the opportunity to, from time to time, go out to a project site, often undeveloped land, and walk it with these experts and learn from them first hand. I loved getting out of the office, and often the project sites were spectacular coastal properties.

As a new associate you always wonder if you're meeting expectations. I tend to be a pretty focused and efficient person, so I was able to achieve and exceed my billable-hour targets each month. Being new to the profession, I was also, of course, concerned about "getting it right". A mistake in law school simply meant a lesser grade but when dealing with real clients a mistake could have serious consequences to others, not to mention the malpractice insurance premium. The learning curve was difficult to measure so I was constantly on my toes.

Following completion of one particularly thorny business deal I assisted on, senior partner Charlie Page scheduled a meeting with me in his office. Scheduled a meeting - not just a casual "come in for second and let's chat" meeting - no, an in writing, on the calendar, official meeting. I had no idea what this meant or if it was normal, but the other associates were mum about it, as if they were nervous for me. The unknown began to dampen my spirit. Mr. Page had a reputation of being a tough but constructive mentor. All of my dealings with him to that point had been positive, and I respected and had learned much from the man. But, there was also the rumor that if you made mistakes on his projects your tenure at the firm could be in jeopardy.

To my relief, when I sat down in his office, Charlie grinned broadly as he presented me with a gift. "A bottle of fine wine for a job well done!" he extolled. I was thrilled, to say the least, and humbly accepted the gift. The praise I received, and especially the wine, was the talk of the office for several days. I was proud to share the story with Lorrie when I got home that evening, but we both wondered what we would do with the wine. Although today we are wine enthusiasts, at that time neither of us drank wine, much less fine wine. So, we decided to just put it on display in the kitchen. About a year later an associate friend asked me how I enjoyed the wine gift I had received from Charlie. Sheepishly I said I wasn't quite sure because we ended up using it in spaghetti sauce and the wine flavor kind of got lost. His face went ashen as his jaw dropped. "What? Don't you know Charlie is a serious connoisseur of wine? If he ever finds out you used the fine wine he gave you in a sauce you'll be a dead man." Of course, he was half joking about the dead man part, but I suddenly realized the gravity of our cooking decision. I resolved to keep my faux pas a secret and did so for 25 years. Long after Charlie had retired, and I was safely ensconced as a partner in the firm, I saw him at a social event. He laughed loudly as I shared the story with him, over a glass of fine wine.

I've practiced in the Land Use arena now for 30 years and can't imagine a more rewarding kind of law. It can be frustrating at times due to the politics involved but overall it's been a pleasure. I have enjoyed working with many sophisticated institutional clients as well as individual homeowners who inadvertently find themselves in a dispute with a neighbor or, worse yet, locked in battle with the California Coastal Commission. I will spare you my plethora of war stories as they would fill an entire book all by themselves. Suffice it to say I have been blessed in my practice and count myself fortunate to have become friends with many of my clients as our relationships have transcended my role as their attorney.

From the very beginning, I was wary of the law's reputation as a "jealous mistress" and I have consistently endeavored to keep her at bay so as not to let the law interfere too much with the real me. That has been a challenge at times as the law is a very demanding profession and, in all honesty, I have acquiesced and adapted in some respects, (e.g. no more baby blue suits). But rather than wholly conform to the mold, over the years I think I've also stretched it a bit ... hopefully for the better. Someone once told me being a Christian lawyer was an oxymoron. I hope my example has shown that statement does not necessarily always have to ring true.

CHAPTER 4 - PACIFIC GROVE

Our love affair with Pacific Grove, which is also known as America's Last Hometown and one of the most romantic cities in the United States, deepened with the passing months and years. Once a Methodist retreat, PG's history is rich with stories of family and God. This, of course, suited us quite well, and I often thought of what it might have been like to live here in days gone by. Our rental house on Ocean View was smack dab in the middle of everything. The PG shoreline is unsurpassed in its beauty with its rocky tidal areas, white sand pocket beaches, walking and bike trail along the bluff top that follows the old Southern Pacific railroad spur out to Spanish Bay, the dazzling hot-pink colored ground cover called "Magic Carpet" that blooms each spring, Lover's Point cove and park, Crespi Pond, Point Pinos Lighthouse, the municipal golf course (known ... locally as "poor man's Pebble Beach" and which is mentioned in the book, "The 50 Golf Courses You Must Play Before You Die"), the historic downtown, the spectacular Victorian mansions converted to bed and breakfast inns, and the clock tower at City Hall that rings the noon chime each day and plays Christmas carols in

December. Perhaps most endearing about our town is its people. For the most part, we are small-town folks tucked away in this relatively secluded hamlet by the sea. Living here is almost a back-in-time experience. In jest I sometimes refer to our town as Mayberry (I loved the "Andy Griffith Show"). Like Mayberry's Gomer, Goober, Howard, Aunt Bea, and Barney Fife, our town also has its cast of well-known characters: the former mayor who tools around in a golf cart, the friendly Chamber of Commerce director, the dutiful crossing guard at the school, the retired fire chief turned philanthropist, the fervent environmental activist down the street and the artist lady who lives in her RV by the cemetery. I aspire to join this august group someday as the old man wearing the faded vest covered with souvenir lighthouse patches and carrying a custom carved walking stick who, each day at dawn, walks his dog on the beach while hunting for sea-glass treasure with his lovely blonde wife on his arm.

Across the street from our house were spectacular tide pools. Each Sunday after church, Lorrie and I would mount Noelle in the kiddie backpack (I think Noelle may have spent more time in that backpack than she did sleeping in her crib) and scamper down the bluff during low tide. Our amazement never ceased. All manner of sea creatures were on display, including crabs, eels, rock fish and sea stars. Shore birds were abundant such as gulls, cormorants, pelicans, oyster-catchers and sand pipers. In the winter months we watched whales and orcas and dolphins frolic as close as 50 yards from shore. We collected abalone shells that had been discarded by sea otters after they finished their meal. One afternoon Noelle decided to adopt a star fish as a pet. Not knowing any better, we attempted to accommodate. I felt bad for that star fish - and my wife - as it took a week to rid our house of the stench the dying creature left with us. We soon learned about the coast's fragile ecosystem and became somewhat protective of it, even leaving the beautiful abalone shells alone to glimmer in the water. We participated in beach clean-up days and took protection and preservation of our shoreline to heart.

On occasion Noelle would get restless in her backpack and want to get down and play in the water, which we didn't allow because sneaker waves are fairly common. To keep her occupied I invented a little song that we would sing together:

"Otters and sea lions, playing in the ocean; Otters and sea lions, playing in the foam; Otters and sea lions, playing in the ocean, playing in the ocean, cause the ocean's their home. And the sea gulls and the pelicans, and the cormorants, fish off the rocks. And the sea gulls and the pelicans, and the cormorants ... fish off of the rocks!"

We sang that song for hours as we explored God's creation. That little ditty has become one of many "Bridges-isms" for which our family is known in local circles. Our grandchildren now sing the song as well.

One of the things I love most about our shoreline is the multi-sensory experience it provides at dawn, especially on foggy mornings. PG's fog is legendary, but truth be known, it only happens a few months a year during the hottest times of the summer. While some locals complain about it, everyone else in California can't wait to experience its cool refreshment. I like the fog and I think it is both romantic, and mystical. Another unique sensory experience is sound travel. At times, and for reasons I've yet to comprehend, a combination of factors come together to enable sound to travel amazing distances around the Point Pinos area. The buoy bell that marks the southern tip of the Monterey Bay (west of which is the open sea) is over a mile out in the ocean. Yet, on some days, you'd swear it was clanging in our back yard. Another wonderful shoreline sound was the old foghorn that would blow its forlorn song when the fog was so thick the lighthouse beacon could not be seen. Sadly, they've removed that icon.

The fragrances of the beach can also be spectacular and often remind me of one of my early boyhood coastal experiences. One summer, while in Portland visiting my grandparents, our family drove to the nearby town of Oceanside, Oregon, and rented a room in a cheap motel on the beach for the weekend. I was probably ten years old. I was so excited to go exploring that I got up long before anyone else and slipped out of the room and down to the shoreline to collect agates on the beach.

As the sun slowly burned off the early morning marine layer, the richness and wetness of the air hung heavy. I could smell and even taste the salty mist. It was like being enveloped in a cloud. I wondered if heaven might be like this. When the urge for sandy beach time would hit, we would stroll down to Lover's Point, originally called Lovers of Jesus Point but altered for political correctness (I really don't like political correctness). The park includes a grassy area with barbecue spots and picnic tables, some local artist sculptures, a burger stand, a children's swimming pool (where all of our children learned how to swim), a small breakwater where the teenagers sunbathe, a kayak concession and a volleyball court. The volleyball court is where an old salt water pool used to be. Back in the 40s when the pool's intake piping rusted out and became too expensive to maintain, they decided to fill the pool with sand. If you dig down deep enough (about 24 inches) you can find the old concrete pool deck. For years, each Sunday afternoon at the randomly and just-for-fun selected time 3:17 p.m., we would meet with a small group of friends to play volleyball. While the children sat just outside the court and made sand castles, the adults pretended we were Olympic volleyball stars.

Soon after settling in PG, Lorrie and I set out to find a church home. A friend recommended a historic church near the downtown. It was called Mayflower, and it had a grand old pipe organ. The congregation was very welcoming and the children's ministry team made us feel comfortable about leaving little Noelle in their care. As usual, we volunteered to serve in the music ministry and once again soon found ourselves leading worship during Sunday morning services. As we met other Christians in town, we also re-instituted our weekly home Bible study. It was a small group at first but quickly grew to twelve. One of the couples drove all the way in from Carmel Valley each week. Devoted fellowship was just what we were looking for.

About the time we were settling into a routine with church and Bible study along came our second child, Whitney Page. As the final weeks of Lorrie's pregnancy approached, trepidation began to set in for me. I could not help but recall the trauma that had surrounded Noelle's birth three years earlier.

When Noelle was born in the spring of our second year of law school, there was no hospital to speak of in Davis, so we had to drive to the nearby town of Woodland when it came time to deliver Noelle. One afternoon when Lorrie was three weeks overdue, we went to see her doctor for what we thought would be a routine checkup … it was far from routine. The doctor told us Noelle was in fetal distress due to the lateness of the term, and he recommended we go straight to the hospital. We were ill-prepared to go to the hospital right then, so on the way we stopped by a market to pick up some essentials ... a change of clothes for Lorrie, some food for me and a toothbrush.

After checking Lorrie in, the hospital staff immediately hooked Noelle up to a heart rate monitor by reaching into the womb and attaching a probe to her tiny head. Though a bit invasive they said this was the most accurate way to monitor the baby's well-being. Lorrie's labor was painfully slow and relatively non-productive. The doctors began to fret. About 9 p.m., while we were breathing through a contraction, the heart rate monitor attached to Noelle suddenly sounded an alarm. I looked up and the line on the monitor went "flat". Thinking the worse, I screamed out for assistance. The nurse arrived promptly but seemed rather nonchalant about the life-and-death emergency. She calmly invited me to take a seat and then proceeded to work on Lorrie. Less than a minute later, she said, "There we go, the monitor just fell off the baby ... happens all the time". Happens all the time? I lost a year off my life during those few minutes.

An hour later the doctors came in and told us they were going to need to perform a Caesarean section on Lorrie. They hastily began preparations while I panicked. I got to a phone and called two friends and asked them to call various prayer chains. Twenty minutes later the doctors arrived all suited up and ready to whisk Lorrie away for surgery. When they checked her dilation one final time, they both expressed shock to see she had progressed from four to ten centimeters and was ready to deliver naturally. Fifteen minutes later we were parents.

So, I wondered what we might be in for during our second birthing experience. Lorrie had a "false alarm" about two o'clock in the afternoon. We drove half way to the hospital before she announced what she thought had been contractions were actually not the real deal. Disappointed, we turned around and went home. Nothing much seemed to happen after that, so I told Lorrie I was going to go play a little volleyball to take the edge off while we waited. That was an exceedingly dumb move by me. The moment I left, Lorrie went into real labor. Although I was a mere half-mile away at Lover's, in the age before cell phones Lorrie had no way of reaching me. When I returned about 90 minutes later, Lorrie was in heavy labor and seemed ready to deliver the baby right there in the house. We grabbed our things and made the second run of the day to the hospital. As soon as we arrived, practically out of breath and in a mild state of panic, the contractions subsided again. They checked us in anyway and we waited and labored until late into the night.

I say "we" labored half tongue-in-cheek because Lorrie is always quick to remind me that in the process of childbirth, the man does very little. But I thought I worked pretty hard at it. Lorrie had low back labor so I was massaging her spine with a tennis ball and breathing intently with her -- "Hee-Hee-Who; Hee-Hee-Who." I worked so hard that I hyperventilated and passed out on top of her. My embarrassment was obvious when I came to and the nurses were all about "me" instead of my laboring bride. After some smelling salts and a few minutes with the proverbial paper sack, I was back in action none the worse for wear except for my bruised ego. Other than "my" labor that night, Whitney's birth seemed to me rather uneventful, at least compared to Noelle's.

As much as we loved the Ocean View house, it became cramped after Whitney arrived. We decided it was time to start looking for something a bit more family friendly. By this time, we had paid off the law school student loans and even saved a little toward a down payment on a house. In the middle of town, near the high school, but a long way from the beach, we found a small house for sale on a quaint little street called Rosemont. The house was only about 950 square feet, but it had three bedrooms (each barely large enough to contain a bed and a dresser) and one-and-a-half baths. The half bath was so small that if someone was in it, whether standing or sitting, you couldn't open or close the door. But to us it seemed perfect.

We negotiated several times with the seller. When we reached the absolute top price we could hope to afford we went to see her to present our final offer. It was early evening. We pulled up in the Honda, parked and then prayed before going in. As we sat down with the seller at her small kitchen table, she graciously offered us some hot cocoa, including Noelle. This made our precocious three-year-old feel quite like an adult so Noelle proceeded to engage in conversation. After a few minutes of banter, Noelle paused, looked our hostess right in the eye and asked with the deepest sincerity, "Are you fat?" Horror of horrors! The lady was a bit overweight but, I mean, oh gosh, uh ... how were we going to cover for this? But before we could say anything, the lady smiled at Noelle and said, "Yes, dear, a little bit, but I'm dieting so I'm trying to address that." We kind of gave her that look that says, "Sheesh, don't kids just say the funniest things?" Assuming our purchase was now in serious jeopardy, we nervously laughed, and I suggested Lorrie take the kids out to the car. Miraculously, our offer was accepted, and just like that, we became home owners.

We moved in about a month later. The inside of the house had been cleaned up pretty well with new paint and new carpet, but the outside was a total mess. We started work in the back yard. We stripped the place down and planted a small lawn and garden patch. There was not a lot of space to deal with, but we wanted it to be safe and comfortable for the kids. The one bonus amenity the house included was an old hot tub built down into a barely safe wooden deck. The tub was heated by a separate hot water heater located in the small one-car garage. The only problem was that it took about 45 minutes to heat up before using it. I was always game to take a dip when I got home and would turn the water heater on around 8 p.m., but by the time we had the girls in bed for the night and the spa was finally warmed up, I was usually too bushed to enjoy it.

Once in a while, however, we would soak in the spa during the day. One weekend afternoon we invited some friends over to join us. We had been working on a few odds and ends projects that week, including an errand to buy and hide outside an "emergency" key. We also replaced a cracked window which happened to face the spa. We put the girls down for a nap, got into our swim suits and settled in for some "spa time". Just as we got in the water, a wind kicked up and the back door to the house slammed shut. The noise startled Whitney, and we could hear her crying over the baby monitor we had brought outside with us. Lorrie stepped out of the spa and grabbed a towel to go inside and tend to the baby when she stopped cold and with a slightly quivering voice nearly screamed, "The door is locked! Where is the hide-a-key?" Well, I hadn't quite gotten around to hiding it and as a matter of fact, it was sitting right there in plain view on the kitchen table ... inside the house ... behind the locked door. We were locked out of the house. This fact raised Lorrie's anxiety level even higher as the baby continued to whine through the monitor. Of course, Whitney and Noelle were perfectly safe, but their well-being suddenly became a crisis for Lorrie.

Everyone got out of the spa. The other ladies consoled Lorrie as if the children were about to breathe their last breath while the men huddled together to solve the dilemma. The solution seemed surprisingly easy. The window putty was still moist from the previous day's replacement, so we figured we'd just scrape it all out, remove the new window and crawl in. All was going well until, just as we began extracting the glass, it cracked and broke in two. Our brand new window was gone. In the scheme of things, it wasn't really a big deal, but after spending every last penny we had to buy the place, a $50 window seemed a very big deal at that moment. But, at least, access to the house had been achieved, and the children were rescued from the brink of their near-death experience.

As a first time homeowner, I made more mistakes than I could count, or wanted to remember. After we finished the backyard landscaping, we turned to the front yard. Located near the front door, was an old decrepit water softening unit that had long since been abandoned. It was an unsightly piece of odd and rusty plumbing equipment, so I determined to remove it. I mean, how hard could that be? Because it was connected to the water main, I dutifully turned off the main. Good thinking and well done, I told myself. Next I went to disconnect the equipment. Of course, after God only knows how many years of sitting there unused, the fittings wouldn't budge. So, I got in the car and drove downtown to the local hardware store, where I met the owner, Bill. I calmly relayed my plight, and he explained how I could overcome the problem. It all sounded simple enough, so I returned home with the correct tool in hand and removed the fittings. But then I realized I had forgotten to get a new pipe to bridge the gap in the line where the equipment had been. Two more trips back and forth to see Bill netted me a hopelessly unresolved problem.

It was getting dark, and the water main was still off. Lorrie was getting a bit edgy as she wanted to bathe the girls and fix dinner. I arrived at PG Hardware (for the fourth time) about 5 minutes after the store had closed for the day. Bill saw me standing at the door looking tired and worn. Taking pity on me, he unlocked the door and invited me in. He grabbed a bag and walked around the store tossing every possible pipe and pipe fitting into the bag and then said, "Come on, let's go fix this." So, on a Sunday night, after hours, the local hardware store owner came to my house and, while I held a flash light, taught me a few of the finer points of plumbing and fixed my pipes. It was an unprecedented house call from the hardware guy. Bill refused my offer to pay him for his above and beyond service, and said, "That's just what we do here in PG; we help each other." Needless to say Bill became one of my heroes that day, and I think I have since single-handedly sent more than

100 customers to him by retelling this story. You've just got to love Pacific Grove.

The previous owner of our house must have been obsessed with Mars because the front yard landscape looked like the surface of the mysterious Red Planet: harsh, dusty, and covered with red lava rock. The only thing resembling an earthly influence was a mangy and very prickly old pine tree planted in the middle of the yard. It was some exotic species that grew out more than it grew up. It was just horrible. I labored for several weekends removing the lava rock but after consulting with the local nursery, I learned we could never grow grass under that tree. So, I decided I'd try my hand at trimming and shaping the sprawling menace, hoping to open up the ground underneath and maybe create something I could stand to look at. Sadly, my arborist skills were found severely lacking, and I ended up with something that would be rejected as ugly even on Mars. After my hatchet job, there was no saving the tree. It had to come out.

Pacific Grove prides itself on its "urban forest" so to remove a tree requires effort akin to an act of Congress. Well, not quite, but a discretionary permit is required. I submitted an application to the City Beautification Committee which scheduled a site visit to see our tree, or what was left of it. Being a land-use lawyer I anticipated how this might unfold, so I planned accordingly. We would angle for sympathy. I would be away at work and Lorrie would greet them. I suggested she stand on the front stoop, barefoot and holding both girls while displaying a pleading look. Her speech was to be simple and to the point, "We need space for our little ones to play, but they cut themselves on the lava rocks that used to be here and we can't grow grass under this tree. My husband tried to trim it, but obviously he didn't do a very good job. Please help me."

Two large vans came to a stop in front of the house and 11 elderly people with matching blue windbreakers - and some with complimenting blue hair - stepped out. They greeted Lorrie and the girls, heard Lorrie's plea and then walked around the tree several times, scratching their heads, rubbing their chins and taking copious notes. They walked up and down the street, viewing the situation from every possible vantage point and taking photos. Then, with a quick wave goodbye, they piled back into their vehicles and were off to their next site visit. A week later we learned their verdict. Our tree removal permit was approved by the narrowest of margins, a 6-5 vote. I chalked this up as one of my most important land-use victories to date.

Although we missed being able to walk across the street to get to the beach, living in the middle of town had some advantages, or at least distinctive. We were fairly close to a wonderful park called George Washington Park (though I'm not sure why, I don't think the former president ever visited California). It was a paradise for kids with a tot lot, swings, a Little League baseball field and lots of room to run and explore. The neighbors were all wonderful. They were either young families like us or elderly couples enjoying their empty nests. The wildlife was also interesting. Instead of whales and pelicans, we had raccoons and parrots. The flock of tropical parrots, which was fabled lore in PG, was obviously not native to the area. As the story went, the colorful and noisy flock got its start several years earlier when two birds escaped their cage and decided to populate the town in celebration of their freedom. On almost any given day you could watch these spunky creatures flit from tree to tree making a most interesting squawking racket.

As endearing as the parrots were, we came to disdain the raccoons. They are nasty and dangerous critters. A friend, who was attacked by one while walking her dog, had to undergo a year of shots to prevent rabies. We trained our girls to avoid them at all cost. One night we heard one scratching around on our roof near the back door. Lorrie and I devised a plan of attack. I stealthily snuck out the door and grabbed the hose. I turned the nozzle head to jet stream. I told Lorrie to turn on the light when I gave her the signal, and I would blast the intruder right between the eyes. It was a good plan except Lorrie neglected to close the door behind me and as I raised the jet stream toward the menace on the roof, she received an unwelcome soaking. In all the commotion the beady-eyed culprit escaped with nary a drop of water on its whiskers. Note to self: don't squirt the wife with the jet stream.

Our town hosts many unique events throughout the year. On a Saturday morning in early October, the downtown becomes sanctuary to hundreds of monarch butterflies.

Actually, hundreds of school children dressed as monarch butterflies. Among its many monikers, Pacific Grove is also known as Butterfly Town USA. The regal monarchs winter in a grove of pine and eucalyptus trees at the west end of town. For several months, hundreds of thousands of the winged beauties cover the trees and fill the air. To celebrate this migration, the elementary schools host a parade through the downtown. The high school marching band lead the processional in full regalia followed by a 1950s vintage police car polished to perfection. The younger children then follow, grouped by class, wearing their orange monarch wings and carrying bags of candy to toss to the spectators. It is all grand fun, which culminates in a community picnic on the field behind Robert Down School.

In December, one neighborhood up on the hill goes all out with yuletide decorations. The area is officially known as "Candy Cane Lane". It is a spectacular place to see Christmas lights, to stroll through the little community park while listening to carolers and to pay a quick visit to Santa. Following Christmas Eve church service, driving through Candy Cane

Lane on the way home has become part of our family tradition.

Another annual PG spectacle is the Feast of Lanterns. This one is hard to describe. It is a week-long festival at the end of July, during which an odd amalgamation of events takes place, including a street dance, a dog parade, arts and crafts booths, concerts, and the grand finale on Saturday: the Feast at Lover's Point. The Feast is basically an all-day picnic culminating with a live play performed on the breakwater that is sort of a Chinese version of Romeo and Juliet. Romeo is represented by a young fellow named Chang, while Juliet is Princess Topaz. There is a royal court of young ladies each with their own gem name, who aspire to someday become Topaz, the star of the show. After the young lovers escape the menacing Mandarin King, a giant sea dragon floating in the cove blows great puffs of smoke to conceal the two as they are swept away in a skiff to safety and a happily-ever-after life. Of course, they then become monarch butterflies and fly away together, only to return each year to winter in PG. Festive oriental lanterns are carried by everyone and the beach is a glow with multi-colored lights as the sun sets. After the young lovers fly away the sky is lit up like the Fourth of July ... literally ... as a grand fireworks show is presented.

The Feast is so popular that getting a seat is a major ordeal. Nearly 15,000 people attend each year (nearly half the town's residents along with an equal number of visitors) and jockey for space on the beach and along the nearby bluffs to watch the event unfold. One year I went down early - as in 3 a.m. - and spread blankets to secure a prime spot on the beach. These days, such place-saving starts days in advance. It is always funny to watch the unknowing visitors who arrive late on Saturday, when the place is already packed, and to see their glee when they spot open sand on the beach. They hustle down near the water's edge thinking they won the lottery to get such a perfect front row seat so late in the day. They spread all their paraphernalia out - blankets, umbrellas, picnic gear, and lawn chairs - and get all settled in for the evening show ... until. Depending on the year and the moon, once in a while as the sun sets the tide begins to rise. Ever so slowly it creeps up on the beach with every other lap of wave. With no beach behind them available to back up onto (the locals have had that ground

staked out for days, and its occupied shoulder-to-shoulder), it is quite a "pre" show to watch their desperate attempts to build sand walls and drainage channels to try to stave off the inevitable encroachment of the sea.
Eventually even the most robust visitors give up, gather their soaking wet gear and trudge up the stairs to try to watch a peek of the show from the street. At least they still get to enjoy the fireworks.

In addition to its spectacular coast line, Pacific Grove also boasts a unique hiking trail locally known as the "green belt". It follows the same railroad right of way that became the bike path along the coastline. At Lover's Point the right of way heads away from the water and winds its way through the golf course and then between residential neighborhoods. This magical place of forested trail in the middle of town is popular with kids on bikes and dog walkers. It is a very busy place, except when warning signs go up after a mountain lion is spotted thinning out the local herd of coastal deer. There has never been an attack on a human, but no one wants to tempt fate. The green belt ends near the Spanish Bay Resort, which was a sand mine back in the 1920s and 1930s. Great, 40-foot-high white silica sand dunes used to comprise the landscape, but they have since all but disappeared having been harvested to make glass. The only true remnant of this bygone time is Asilomar State Beach, a 200-foot-wide, quarter-mile long strip of white sand at the extreme south end of town. It is a popular surfing spot and one of the last places evening bonfires are permitted on the beach. Dogs run free at Asilomar as do the kids. Our children loved this particular beach for boogie boarding and roasting marshmallows. It tends to be mostly a locals beach because there are no restroom facilities, which Lorrie is always complaining about, but I think enhances the charm of the place.

After two years in our little Rosemont house, we became pregnant for the third time and had to again entertain moving to a larger place. Fortunately, the real estate market had been on an upswing so we had a bit of equity available to help us consider a bigger house. We expected this would be our last child and so we hoped to move into a house we could call home forever. Even though we had some equity built up, we were sad to discover what little it could actually buy. We hunted for a house for weeks and in the process saw some of the most bizarre homes you can imagine. Some rivaled the famed San Jose "Mystery House". One I remember distinctly had three bedrooms but no hallway, so to get to the back bedroom you had to walk through the other two. It was classic Pacific Grove.

One Sunday afternoon, after returning from a weekend family camping trip in the nearby Santa Cruz Mountains, I opened the local newspaper to scan the real estate section. To my surprise there was a new listing in the most coveted neighborhood in town known as the Beach Tract, which was down by the golf course, lighthouse and Point Pinos. Even more surprising was that the asking price was only slightly above the top of our range. I suspected the price was a typo but decided to run down to see the house anyway since it was listed as "open" until 4 p.m. that day. When I arrived, I immediately realized the price was not a typo. It was a classic case of the worst house in the best neighborhood. As I walked through, despite the pitiful condition of the place, I saw that the "bones" seemed solid and the floor plan was perfect. The two-story house had four bedrooms, three bathrooms, a small dining area and a bonus "family" room in the back. The lot was huge (for Pacific Grove that means 0.2 acres), and the views of the water from the upstairs master bedroom were astounding. The house was "second" row, just one row behind Ocean View Boulevard, and the beach was a mere 3-minute walk around the block. Before going home to get Lorrie I stopped by to see a friend who was savvy about PG real estate. He had "flipped" numerous homes before he settled in an amazing golf course frontage house with unobstructed bay views. He was available to swing by the house with me, and, after a quick viewing, he said he would buy it if I didn't. That was all the endorsement I needed, so I quickly went home to pack up the girls and haul them down to see the "Surf" - Surf Avenue - house. Lorrie, who was exhausted from the camping adventure and newly pregnant, was hesitant as we walked through the front door. I think she may have been having flash backs to Americana Arms, but I dragged her in and spoke to her of all the "potential" I saw. All she saw was "work" written in bold letters across the front of the house and in every room. Absolutely nothing about the house attracted her, until I got her upstairs where even she was impressed with the bay views from the master bedroom window.

We submitted an offer the next day and were in escrow within a week. During my due diligence investigation (reviewing the City's records on the property), I learned several disturbing facts. The place had been "ticketed" by City zoning enforcement officials for operation as an illegal motel/flop house. We later learned the place had been used as a half-way house for drug addicts. We also learned the place was full of asbestos, from the popcorn ceiling to much of the old 1960s linoleum that covered the floors. The waste-water had to be pumped "up slope" through an underground sump pump station in the front yard that made quite a racket when it went off. The electrical panel was shot, and the windows, several of which were broken, were paper thin. The back deck was rotting, the driveway had huge cracks and the landscape hadn't been touched in decades. The roof leaked and the paint was pealing. To Lorrie's credit, her assessment of the work to be done and consequent caution had been more than accurate. The Tom Hanks movie called, "The Money Pit" came to mind. I wondered if I would fare as well in the starring role as Hanks had.

After closing escrow, we spent two months working on the house before we could move in. We had been able to negotiate the price down from asking and so had a little money to pay for some modest repairs. A contractor friend from church and his crew did somewhat of a miracle makeover to the house. It was mostly aesthetic work, but they made the place safe and livable. The asbestos was removed by men in moon suits and hauled away to a hazardous waste facility in Nevada. The 1960s-style "sunken" living room floor was raised to align with the rest of the house. The three-foot-wide tile path that snaked from the front door through the living area to the kitchen was torn up and replaced with new carpet. The entire place was painted, inside and out. We spent three days scrubbing the grime off the kitchen and the bathrooms. The attic crawl space was insulated, twice.

I was very careful to schedule the various work crews so they wouldn't conflict with each other. On the day the electrician was installing a new panel and doing some related wiring in the attic, an insulation company, not the one I had hired, arrived and started blowing insulation into the attic with a huge tube machine. The electrician yelled and screamed as he emerged from the attic cursing, spitting and covered with blown insulation. I received an urgent call at the office and had to break away and drive over to address the confusion. The insulation guy had been one of the first to give me a bid, but I never heard from him again. He never followed up, so neither did I, and I hired another company. He sheepishly gave me that "Gee whiz, Wally" look and said he thought he had been hired. I showed him my prepaid contract with the insulation company I had hired (and who was scheduled to arrive the next day) and asked him where his contract was, knowing of course that he didn't have one. He just kind of shrugged, stuck his hands in his pockets and whistled a signal for his crew to withdraw. Without so much as a word, they all packed up and then drove away. No apology, no goodbye, not another word, they just disappeared.

Fortunately, I was able to get a partial refund from the prepaid insulation company I had hired since more than half the work had been done by the unscheduled crew. When the job was finished and my hired fellow was paid and satisfied, I tried to reach the uninvited company to offer them partial payment for the work they had done (albeit without my permission). I called several times and left several messages but the guy never called back. So, we enjoyed a 50 percent discount on our insulation. With that and a few other cost savings we scraped out along the way, we were able to replace, instead of just repair, the roof. Hallelujah!

And so it went. For two months the house was a bustle of activity. We met several of our neighbors during that time, and to a person, they were ecstatic about our purchase of the house and all the work being done to it. The transition from drug addict flop house to family home was welcomed by all. When the work was done, my contractor friend sighed, smiled and shook his head. "You know John, I think you've got a nice place here, but I don't think the person who built it knew much about construction or carpentry. I've really never seen anything quite like this place, but somehow it works." Over the years many more projects would have to be done. The house will never be a palace, and compared to the regal estate homes of some of my colleagues in the legal profession, our house wouldn't be considered much more than a beach shack, but it's our beach shack and I love it. Lorrie, and I learned contentment early in our married life and that lesson has served us well. We were just as happy living off free-will offerings with Hosanna and loans in law school as we have been with a comfortable lawyer's salary. We've just never been very much about fancy things.

The November following our move to the Surf house our girls got a little brother. Grant Sterling was born, and our quiver was full. A few weeks before his arrival the San Francisco and Monterey Bay areas suffered a massive earthquake. It hit just after 5 p.m. while I was at work. I remember my reflex to the shaker was to dive under my desk and cover my head with my hands. I guess all those years of duck-and-cover drills in elementary school stuck with me. On a normal day my drive home from the office took about 20 minutes. With all the power out in town and the aftershocks still rattling the area, I decided driving home via the normal route, through Monterey and along the shoreline, might be impossible, so I decided to take the longer but less traveled, back way, through and over the Aquajito. It was a brilliant idea, conceptually. What I hadn't counted on, were the fallen boulders and trees that would litter the narrow, winding two-lane country road. Oh, I missed the traffic snarls in town all right, but it took me almost an hour to maneuver around all the mountain debris. Fortunately, nothing completely closed the road. While I painstakingly drove home, my mind was racing. I knew Lorrie was due to deliver our third child any day, and I was afraid the shock of everything might cause her to go into early labor. Would the hospital have power? Was it even still standing?

As I picked my way over the mountain I listened to a talk radio station out of San Francisco for minute-by-minute news updates. A section of the Bay Bridge had collapsed, fires raged in downtown San Francisco, Oakland was in shambles, and parts of Candlestick Park, where game three of the World Series was being played that night, had crumbled. As I listened my anxiety and concern for my family grew. Thoughts of tsunami began to creep into my mind. Lord, why did I have to buy a house so close to the water! Would my whole world be washed out to sea?

By the time I reached our driveway, I was a basket case. Tears fell freely down my cheeks and my breathing slowed a bit when I saw the house was still standing. I didn't see any broken glass or even any downed power lines. I raced to the front door and burst into the house like a half-wild man. Lorrie and the girls were calmly and safely huddled on the couch reading a book together. Other than the power being out, the house was perfectly sound. "Hi hon, did you hear about the earthquake?" Lorrie calmly asked as she greeted me with a fairly normal welcome home hug. "Uh, yes," I replied. We had been spared from the great quake.

In my romantic future-world, the Surf house (once referred to in an old newspaper article as "The Gray Ghost") will someday be passed on to our kids, who I hope will agree to keep it as a family beach retreat for the grands and the greats to enjoy. It will serve as a kind of legacy, a tangible sign or marker that the Bridges family would always belong in Pacific Grove. Markers, especially memorial markers, are important to me as a way to speak to future generations. My father's father, after whom I am named Sterling (as are my son and grandson), died when my dad was only eight years old. He is buried in a small rural cemetery at the end of a rough and pothole challenged dirt road outside Zebulon, North

Carolina. All I ever knew of him were the few memories my dad could recall and the epitaph carved into his graveside monument stone. It is an excerpt from a famous poem written by Sam Walter Foss, " ... let me live in my house by the side of the road and be a friend to man." My dad's newly placed marker (September 9, 2015) in Billings, Montana, bears those same words, a noble aspiration indeed. Though I never met Grandpa Bridges, I've always felt I knew him by virtue of those few words. Perhaps my progeny will someday know something of me by coming to the Surf house.

If not, perhaps they'll know of me by visiting my grave marker, which will someday be placed about three blocks south of the Surf house, in El Carmelo cemetery. Yes, Lorrie and I already have a plot there. It is approximately 400 paces due east of Point Pinos Lighthouse, and at night you can see the great beacon filtered through the cypress trees. My kids think it strange and maybe even a bit morbid that I have such a plot of ground, and even more so the fact that I took them there to stand on it with me while I was still alive and well. With absolute confidence and assurance, I know when I leave this earth

I will reside eternally in heaven with my Savior. But I simply told them that here, in El Carmelo, my marker will stand as evidence of my love for God, my love for them, and my love for Pacific Grove.

CHAPTER 5 - TO BUILD A CHURCH

As we gradually became full-fledged members of the Monterey Peninsula community, my amazement at the countless blessings I was experiencing grew. I was saved by grace, happily married to a beautiful and loving wife, father of three wonderful children, surrounded by friends and vibrant fellowship, enjoying good health, learning at and working in a good job with an excellent law firm, settled into a wonderful town, and owning a home a half-block from the beach. It was hard to imagine a more idyllic situation. The phrase "exceedingly abundantly beyond" came to mind often. I was, of course, grateful to God and my heart overflowed with thanksgiving. I never for a moment forgot how all of this had come to pass. I knew with certainty that God brought us here and that our only role in the process had been obedience to His direction. The "how" we got here was clear, but the "why" remained a mystery.

I was fortunate to grow up in a loving family, so naturally I had desired the same. And who, if they were honest, wouldn't want to live near the beach? But working as a lawyer had never been in my plan. It had never been something on my "list". Some people grow up dreaming about being a lawyer, but not me. Sure I'd seen Perry Mason a time or two as a kid, but that's about as close to knowing what a lawyer was as I had ever gotten. The whole law school path had been completely unforeseen. While I understood it was not some random cosmic kismet and that omniscient God was clearly leading the way, I still struggled to comprehend the why of it. Of all the paths God could have directed me to follow (and I would have followed any path He chose for me), why this one and why to here? Although I was far too engaged in the fullness of everything I was experiencing to spend much time pondering this question, it nevertheless lingered in the back of my mind.

Since my job was obviously not a ministry, at least not as I had imagined Hosanna might have been, I concluded it must just be a means to an end. As the Apostle Paul made tents to support his ministry endeavors, I would practice law. But what was my ministry purpose to be? My family, of course; my local church community, sure; but was that it? Was there nothing of a more profound nature or grander scheme? If not, I would be satisfied serving in whatever capacity God ordained. But, still, in light of the magnitude of the course change after college and the time and effort I had devoted to my legal training, it just seemed there should be something more for me to do.

About a year after we began attending Mayflower Church, a new start-up church emerged in town. It had grown from a home Bible study group into a congregation of about 50 people. It was associated with a church in southern California I had heard about called Calvary Chapel. The new church's pastor was a young man, about our age, named Bill Holdridge. Having outgrown the small meeting room at the local community center, the fledgling church was looking for a place to meet on Sundays, and Mayflower invited them to use their building on Sunday afternoons.

During college the church I attended was what most would call an evangelical non-denominational church. The focus was on teaching the Bible, verse-by-verse, rather than preaching about themes or topics. This style of church was very attractive to me, and I missed it because the pastor at Mayflower (Cliff) was more of a thematic preacher than a Bible teacher. Lorrie and I were both intrigued by Calvary's verse-by-verse teaching style, but three things prevented us from changing churches. We had grown into a position of responsibility at Mayflower in terms of leading worship; our kids needed to nap on Sunday afternoon; and for me, I tend to be an intensely loyal person. I had cast my lot with Mayflower, and I was not one to church hop.

Several months later Calvary moved its meeting place a few blocks up the street to the new theater in the downtown. They started meeting at 9 a.m. on Sunday mornings and would wrap things up just as the popcorn smell would begin to waft through the place for the Sunday matinee. Since Mayflower's main service was at 11 a.m., Lorrie and I decided to treat Calvary as our "Sunday school". We would get our dose of verse-by-verse expositional Bible teaching at 9a.m. and then attend church at Mayflower at 11 a.m. In addition to the Bible teaching we longed for, Calvary also introduced us to a whole new group of people, many of whom were young families like us.

Our two pastors, Cliff and Bill, were good friends, and the fact of our dual church attendance quickly became apparent (not that we tried to conceal it from anyone). Doing both services with a quick sound check and music rehearsal in between made for long Sunday mornings, especially for the kids, but we made it work and were enjoying all of it. One Sunday after church, Cliff asked us to lunch. We had grown to love and admire this servant of God and were thrilled at the opportunity to have lunch and hopefully deepen our relationship with him. After sandwiches and small talk, Cliff took on a more serious tone. He shared about how much he respected Bill's teaching and how happy he was that Calvary's congregation was growing. We chimed in that we loved Bill's teaching and that we had grown up in that style of church and how blessed we felt to be able to attend Calvary and Mayflower at the same time. It was really a best of both worlds from our perspective. Cliff smiled at our exuberance. I think he understood our hearts and the fact that we were genuine in our praise of both churches. I think he also had a sense about the extent of my loyalty toward him and our Mayflower family. But, he then explained how he didn't feel right about having us serve in leadership at Mayflower if we weren't "all in" in every respect.

As the conversation unfolded I was struck by the wisdom of what Cliff was saying and a bit embarrassed that in my zeal to serve and all my crazy busyness, I had never paused long enough to consider it. As the conversation drew to a close, with a tinge of both sadness and encouragement in his voice, Cliff said he thought perhaps we should make Calvary our church home. At first I thought, "Is he asking us to leave?" But then, as I played his comment over again in my mind, I realized, no, Cliff was inviting us to follow after our hearts' desire. He was removing my self-imposed tether to Mayflower, almost like releasing a bond servant. I was dumbstruck.

We had experienced myriad types of churches while touring with Hosanna, but one thing seemed fairly constant: churches were always conscious about maintaining and growing membership. But Cliff wasn't about that at all. He was about ensuring that we were spiritually satisfied and filled to the brim. He realized that his preaching style was not going to accomplish that for us. He knew that deep down we longed for something different than he could provide. He loved us enough to let us go. I was humbled by the greatness of this man and by his heart for our well-being.

Lorrie and I prayed over this "invitation" and, after a few more conversations with both Cliff and Bill, we made the move. Of course, we continued in fellowship with our friends at Mayflower and would even occasionally visit and serve when needed on the worship team for Sunday evening services. The theater had no Sunday school rooms for kids during the service, so Calvary rented a portion of Mayflower's building they didn't use. So, physically we were still at Mayflower every Sunday, dropping off and picking up our children. The transition was smooth and seamless. Thereafter, I lost track of how many times I thanked Cliff for relieving me of my self-imposed fetter, and every time I did he would just give me a big grin and a fatherly bear hug and tell me how much he loved me.

True to form, Lorrie and I jumped into ministry opportunities at Calvary with both feet. Lorrie plugged into the children's ministry, and I was asked to serve on the Board of Directors. We were both invited to join the worship team. For the first time we found ourselves teamed up with musicians far superior to and more experienced than ourselves. It was freeing to be a team member rather than a team leader for a change. My gift of songwriting also began to flourish again, and I wrote dozens of songs, many of which the Calvary team collaborated on arranging, and together we used for church worship. Others of my new songs were enjoyed in our home Bible study group, which also grew in number and maturity.

The theater Calvary met in was a four-plex. In the largest room we held church, the smallest was reserved for mothers with babies and the other two were used by the middle school and high school groups respectively. We had to arrive about an hour early each Sunday to help set up the sound system and run through a quick rehearsal. We were fairly adept at all of this having been our own roadies with Hosanna. While we set up and rehearsed, Noelle and Whitney would keep busy by reading or chatting with friends. Grant would go "hunting".

Grant had a penchant for hunting any and every thing. His favorite prey was golf balls. Since we lived only a block away from the golf course, Grant and I would regularly walk along the edges of the fairways and in the out-of-bounds areas searching for abandoned balls. It was a rare outing that didn't net at least a few finds, and Grant's golf ball collection grew large. During the hour before church, however, Grant turned his sights on a different target - coins. Theater seats and floors contain a veritable treasure trove of coins for a little boy to find. Because the floor was quite grimy we tried to discourage the foray at first, but Grant would not be dissuaded. So we decided to use the opportunity to teach him a little bit about stewardship and giving. Because it was impossible to return stray coins to theater goers from the night before, we explained it was okay for him to keep his treasure, provided he gave half of the bounty to the Sunday school offering plate. Grant was fine with that. He wasn't about the money, just the hunt. We finally figured out that all would be best served if we just brought along a container of Handi Wipes for his hands, elbows, and knees along with a second outfit of clothes to change into right before church started. Adaptive parenting is essential when raising a little boy.

For such a small congregation, the Board of Directors at Calvary was made up of an impressive array of talent. Two pastors, a financial planner, a loan executive, a contractor, an insurance broker and me, the lawyer. The first task I was given was to re-write the corporate bylaws. Churches in California are technically non-profit corporations, so certain procedures must be followed to be legal in the eyes of the state. The bylaws Calvary had adopted at its inception were copied from a Congregational church that someone had once attended. Little thought had been given to what the document actually said, it was just signed and filed with the Secretary of State in order to check the box on the application form and move on. After reading the bylaws, I met with Bill and explained that Calvary operated differently than these written bylaws. Leadership at Calvary was loosely based on what is known as the Mosaic model. In other words, the Pastor makes all the decisions guided by the advice of a Board of Directors and Elders. In contrast, under the Congregational model, all decisions of any consequence must be formally voted on by the entire congregation. Bill was surprised by this revelation and asked me simply to "fix it to read as we operate." So I did. Ironically, the first and only vote the congregation of Calvary Chapel Monterey Bay ever took was to unanimously adopt new bylaws that eliminated all future congregational voting.

I enjoyed serving on the Calvary Board. One of the more challenging aspects for me was handling benevolence requests (when folks who are short on money ask the church for financial assistance). My heart wanted to grant every request, but fortunately strict criteria had been developed. Perhaps the wisest stipulation was to require recipients of aid to attend a money management and budgeting class. The idea was to teach and empower as well as assist. The annual church budgeting process was another major task. Our church was so small that the budget was pretty slim. I remember individual line items included specific office supply purchases such as paper and pencils. The responsibility for handling tithes and offerings was also eye-opening as there were so many needs and so little money.

As time passed and our kids grew so did the church. Because of the matinee, we couldn't add a later second service so we added an earlier one. This was tough on those involved in the services and especially those who had to set up each Sunday morning. As it became progressively more difficult for us to operate effectively in the confines of the four-plex, the landlord started making noise about wanting us to move out. This presented a serious problem. Finding another space large enough for our burgeoning congregation and all of the children was going to be difficult. A committee of the Board was formed to begin researching options. It became evident fairly quickly that finding a rental space on the Peninsula that was large enough to accommodate our needs and that we could afford would not be possible. So, as many Calvary Chapels had done before us, we started thinking about buying a building. We first looked at warehouse space in nearby Sand City and found a building that might be converted to function as a church. But as we looked closer we learned there was little to no parking available. We later realized this was the norm for warehouse space: plenty of room to meet but only if everyone walked or rode a bike. As pressure from the landlord intensified, our options seemed to dwindle.

Chuck Smith, the founding pastor of the original Calvary Chapel in Costa Mesa, California, was brought in to consult. He had faced this situation with dozens of churches, and his advice was quick, direct, and unqualified: buy a piece of land and build. Easy for him to say, I thought. We were struggling with the idea of rent or a small mortgage on an old building we might convert with sweat equity. Buying land and building a brand-new church seemed, frankly, out of the question. But, nonetheless a decision was made to expand our search parameters to include land. What Chuck perhaps didn't appreciate was the cost of land on the Monterey Peninsula, the fact there was very little water available for new development, and the vigorous no-growth sentiment that seemed to doom almost every project on the Peninsula that came up for review.

Just when it looked like we might be running out of options, a realtor told us about a 7-acre parcel east of town between the highway and the airport and about a mile from my office. It had been on the market for a long time and wouldn't sell due to the difficult politics of the area. Development opposition was fierce. It was often led by a Highway Coalition group that fought additional development in the corridor claiming traffic on the two-lane rural highway already exceeded capacity. They were often joined by the Sierra Club, who was concerned property may be prime habitat for an endangered plant species. And then there was the Airport Land Use Commission that was extremely wary (for safety reasons) of any development proposed in the vicinity of the airport. Worse yet, the property had no direct access and it was zoned industrial (where churches were disallowed).

The Realtor said the owner was desperate to sell and that we should make a low offer and see what happened. We only needed about four acres to build a church adequate to meet our needs so an offer was submitted contingent on getting all necessary approvals to build, including rezoning and a subdivision to split the parcel in two. We crunched the numbers and made a ridiculously low offer that was, in truth, still more than I thought we could legitimately afford. The offer was accepted without debate. Instead of euphoria, a sense of foreboding set in. The Board held meeting after meeting, sometimes late into the evening, in the basement of Mayflower Church to discuss how the land might be financed and, even if it was obtainable, to figure out where in the world money would come from to construct a building. Some suggested, only half in jest, that perhaps we could buy the lot and just erect a big tent.

Knowing firsthand the complexities of the land-use process and the many hurdles necessary to overcome, I became the point person for the project's permitting and legal issues. During our due diligence review of the property, we discovered direct access to the property from the highway would never be allowed due to sight distance and grade problems, and the alternative existing access a quarter-mile to the west had an inadequate easement. Even if the easement issue could be remedied, the cost of constructing and maintaining a new private frontage road would be a significant additional cost burden. Each issue we discovered only added to the improbability of financing. If the theoretical monthly payments were not daunting enough, we had woeful little money saved for the substantial down payment that would be necessary. In sum, the whole idea seemed to border on the impossible.

But Bill thought otherwise. With encouragement from his pastor, Chuck, Bill subscribed to what I dubbed the "Field of Dreams" mind set: "If you build it, they will come." Even though Field of Dreams was one of my favorite movies, I couldn't embrace the notion for the church. Though not mandated under the bylaws, Bill desired the Board of Directors to agree unanimously on big decisions, and this was certainly big. I admired Bill for his restraint, but in this instance it created substantial pressure on me as I found myself to be the lone holdout on the Board. I struggled mightily with this. Was I lacking faith? Was I succumbing to fear? Was I being too temporally minded? Was I being too lawyerly? Should I resign from the Board?

As was so often the case when I wrestled with a difficult decision, I fell back on prayer. I'm not sure why I didn't just automatically go there first as sometimes it seems I'd save myself a lot of grief. So I prayed (and even fasted for a short time) seeking a divine solution. In His ever faithful way, God answered. While reading the Bible I came across a passage in the Gospel of Luke that I'd never really focused on before. In a parable Jesus talked about a man who started a building project before counting the cost and when he was unable to complete the project he became a subject of ridicule in the community.

I met with Bill and shared my revelation with him. I explained that if we could go through an exercise of counting the cost, in other words calculating whether we could complete a church building project before we started one, then I thought I'd have a peace about going forward. To my surprise, Bill agreed without hesitation. My surprise was to see how much Bill valued my input and was willing to act on it. Reflecting back today I sometimes wonder if Bill, already knowing through his own revelation what the outcome would be, agreed to go through with the exercise just to help my unbelief. He always had such a pastor's heart.

So it was decided that a non-binding "pledge of the heart" would be asked of the congregation. After two weeks of explanation and prayer, the congregation received pledge cards in their Sunday morning bulletin. There was a palpable excitement in church that day. The room was abuzz with hope and expectation, as was I. It wasn't exactly a fleece, but it was an opportunity for God to give direction through the actions of His people. When the pledge commitments were tallied, our church family made it abundantly clear they would stand behind a decision to buy the land and build a church. Celebration followed, and a purchase contract was signed. For the next several months, while the "sale-pending" sign was prominently displayed next to the highway, Bill encouraged church members driving by the property to utter a simple prayer for the project: "Grace! Grace!"

For the next several months, we set about the task of resolving all the contract contingencies, which collectively looked about as insurmountable as the walls of Jericho. Among the giant stones in the wall we faced were zoning change, subdivision, use permit, design approval, myriad technical studies, biological constraints, water supply, highway access, California Environmental Quality Act (CEQA) review, road and utility easements, the Airport Land Use Commission (ALUC) and financing. The seller was cooperative regarding a time line to accomplish all of this because there were no other potential buyers. So, the path to approval was defined, and the long difficult march to Jericho began.

My role in the process increased due to my familiarity with the applicable law and politics of the land-use arena. Over the years I had developed good relationships with City of

Monterey staff members, and, after several conversations, they agreed a church would actually be a good use for the land since it would only meet a few days a week (e.g., Sunday and Wednesday) and, with a relatively small number of staff on campus during the rest of the week, water and traffic impacts would likely be less for a church than almost any other use of this property. So, a project application was fashioned that garnered the support of city staff. The only reservation expressed was that a church wouldn't generate tax revenue for the city.

After a series of complex negotiations, we were able to resolve the several easement issues that burdened the title to the land. We also reached accord on highway mitigations by agreeing to participate in the future funding of a traffic light at the access driveway if and when ever it became necessary. We were also able to satisfy CEQA and design around or mitigate the biological constraints on the property. The City had just enough water available in their remaining allocation for institutional uses to cover our need, and they agreed we could have it. A bank was found that would finance both the land and the building, though their willingness to do so remains a mystery to me today because the congregational pledges were intentionally non-binding. In terms of agency approvals, our first stop was the ALUC. This airport commission had very strict rules about buildings near the airport. Schools and day care centers were strictly forbidden. Although churches were not clearly defined as a category of use in their regulations, the ALUC decided that even with the limited numbers of days of use, a church was still an inappropriate activity near the airport and they voted to deny the project. Because their decision could be appealed to the City Council I knew all was not lost...yet.

Our next stop was the City Architectural Review Board ("ARB") and, after several modest design changes, we received our first positive vote. Next, the City Planning Commission weighed in. Normally the Planning Commission is the final approval necessary, but, because of the rezoning component of the application and the ALUC denial, we knew we would have to pay a visit to the City Council. With the ARB approval and the staff support we had garnered at the outset, the Planning Commission was comfortable with the project and approved it.

Then the appeals came in. Both the Highway Coalition and the Sierra Club appealed as I had anticipated they might. As a result, all aspects of the project were going to be subject to City Council review. Because we had mitigated for the highway issues and the biological concerns to staff's satisfaction, I was hopeful we might overcome the two appeals. But with the concern about lost tax revenue Council approval was far from certain. The ALUC denial also loomed large because under state law, we needed a supermajority of the Council members (four of five) to override their denial. This would be a very high hurdle indeed.

The Calvary Board held another special meeting to prepare for the hearing before the City Council. To a person, we all recognized the huge obstacles God had already brought us through, over, and around. I advised that we encourage as many people as could to attend the meeting. Not all would need to speak, but a substantial physical presence would be helpful. I reached out to each of the appellants directly to see if there was any additional mitigation that might satisfy their concerns, but to no avail. I was cautiously optimistic going into the hearing, but if I had learned anything in my years of Land Use practice it was that you should always expect the unexpected.

We were scheduled for the evening portion of the council's Tuesday agenda which was good as it would enable more people to attend because they would be done with work for the day. The group of supporters who arrived that evening was larger than expected. We gathered together before the hearing to pray for God's "Grace" outside on the steps of historic Colton Hall where the City Council met. In that moment, it all seemed so natural, almost ordained. Colton, the first American Alcalde, or mayor, in California who served here in 1846 was himself a pastor, a Navy chaplain. No doubt these steps were familiar with the prayers of the faithful. Moreover, many great things had happened in this hallowed hall, including the first California Constitutional Convention in 1849. We hoped and believed our prayers this night would lead to another great happening.

When the appointed time arrived, we all filed into the council chambers. I had appeared before the Monterey City Council many times to advocate for my clients, but I had never seen such a packed room. Every seat was filled, as were the aisles with people standing shoulder to shoulder. Many more stood outside and craned their necks for a glimpse of the activity inside through the open double doors in the back of the great hall. We had decided it would be best to consolidate our presentation to just a handful of speakers. After the staff presented the project details, the procedural context, and explained the six separate approvals being requested, I stood to approach the podium to speak on behalf of the church.

As I proceeded forward it almost felt as if I was moving in slow motion as my mind flashed back over the past many months of prayer and work. Our march to Jericho was complete. We were now standing before the great walls. It was time to blow the trumpets as they did in the Bible. But my mind didn't stop there: I also flashed back further to my personal journey and suddenly the elusive "why" of it all came clear to me. God had directed each step of my preceding 12 years to culminate with these final few steps to the podium. God's purpose for me, the reason He pulled me away from Montana, the reason He sent me to law school, the reason He brought me to this place ... my ministry ... was this moment.

It was all I could to do to maintain my composure as I began to speak. In that moment I felt the confident assurance of God's hand on my shoulder. I abbreviated my planned remarks about the project's history and the relevant legal points to instead speak contemporaneously about the importance of Calvary Chapel to the future health and well-being of the Monterey Peninsula and how what we could bring to the community would be far more valuable than a few extra tax dollars. When I asked for a showing of who in the audience supported the project, with the exception of the two appellants' representatives, the entire room stood in unison. The very sound of it was impressive. After our other assigned speakers addressed their topics and the appellants presented their cases, I offered a brief rebuttal and then sat down. The public hearing was closed with a crack of the mayor's gavel. After a short recess the meeting was called back to order, and the council's public deliberation began.

Following 20 minutes of questions to staff and discussion on the dais, the mayor invited a motion on the first order of business: the ALUC denial. This was first because unless the council voted to override the ALUC, voting on all the other aspects of the project would be moot. A motion to override the denial and approve the project was made and followed by a second. The Council then debated the motion. It's usually difficult to predict a vote based on such debate because often points are raised just for the sake of making a record of due deliberation. Both the pros and cons of the motion - and the project - were robustly discussed. When all had made their points, the mayor called the question and gave instruction for a roll call vote so that each council member could express his or her vote clearly for the record.

The Mayor spoke, "The motion on the floor is to override the ALUC denial and, in so doing, to find the project consistent with applicable airport land-use regulations. Those in favor signify by saying aye, those opposed, nay." The City Clerk then proceeded to ask each council member, in turn, for their vote: "Aye," "Aye," "Nay," "Aye,".... After the third yes vote was registered, an audible murmur of excitement circulated through the crowd but most did not understand that a 4/5 supermajority vote was required on this item. Per Robert's Rules of Order, the last person to vote was the Mayor, the Alcalde. The elected leader of the City spoke, "Aye!" And with that one word, the single largest foundation stone of Jericho's fortress was broken and the walls began crumbling. Each of the remaining five items requiring Council action was quickly dispatched with unanimous votes. The church project was approved. The total vote tally on all motions combined was 29 ayes and only a single nay.

The chamber erupted in applause. The admonition against such displays that was usually given by the mayor to maintain order and decorum did not follow. This time the mayor, council members and staff all joined in. As the congregation gathered outside, a celebratory mood warmed the cool night air. People seemed to understand the magnitude of what just happened and the miracle they had just witnessed. After a few minutes of revelry, Bill offered a prayer of thanksgiving and then dismissed the crowd. There was still much work to be done, but the board members decided to defer discussion of next steps and to instead just enjoy the moment.

After most had left, Lorrie and I walked back to our car hand-in-hand. When we got into the car and the dome light finally faded, I sat motionless behind the steering wheel. My eyes welled with emotion, but in the dark Lorrie could not see the moistening of my cheeks. After a long minute she put her hand on my shoulder and said, "Babe, we should go, we have to get the babysitter home, are you okay?" I turned to her and nodded and smiled. She now saw my tears but said nothing more. After another pause to regain my composure, I simply said, "This is why I became a lawyer ... to build a church." Lorrie squeezed my hand and whispered, "I know."

When later asked how I felt about the outcome and my role in it, I reflected that it was kind of like experiencing what an orchestra conductor must feel as he witnesses a masterpiece well-performed by many skilled musicians knowing his role was simply to waive a small baton. The City Clerk would later tell me that in all her years on the job, our hearing was the most inspiring she had ever seen. She said, "It felt more like a revival meeting than a council meeting." My hope for our community was that those words might come true and that Calvary Chapel would bring spiritual health and revival to the Monterey Peninsula.

CHAPTER 6 - FATHERHOOD

"Behold, children are a gift of the Lord;
The fruit of the womb is a reward.
Like arrows in the hand of a warrior,
So are the children of one's youth.
How blessed is the man whose quiver
is full of them; ..." (Psalm 127:3-5)

Dad. Next to God, I think this three-letter word has been the most profound in my life. Fatherhood is a great and wonderful mystery. It is a holy calling that is dynamic, demanding, frightening and fulfilling, all at the same time. My children are my progeny, my ministry and my future on earth. I'm not sure exactly when I started learning about being a dad, but I know I'll never stop. I also know that despite my failures and imperfections as a father, God is always available to help me and He is the perfect role model.

At the outset, I must acknowledge that I have been more fortunate than many because in addition to knowing God as my Abba Father (Daddy), I also had a loving father figure here on earth. Simply stated, my dad was a great man, though perhaps not great as the world might measure greatness. He didn't amass a great fortune or invent a culture-changing product, his name does not adorn a building and his life will not likely be noted in many books, other than this one. The greatness of my father (after whom I am named ... "John") was born out of his heart for family. This is especially noteworthy because his father died (from wounds suffered while serving our country in the Great War; a.k.a. World War 1), when he was only eight years old. At that young age, a boy is only beginning to understand what fatherhood looks like. Though he sometimes complained about the doting he endured from his mother, I think my dad learned almost everything about family from her -- the importance of loving, the honor in protecting, and the sacrifice required to provide.

Without necessarily being taught the notion, my dad embraced the Biblical marriage directive to leave and cleave. Dad left his North Carolina roots to marry Mom. He loved my mother deeply, faithfully and completely for the nearly 60 years they were together on this earth. Mom was always his number one priority. After completing four years of service in the Air Force, the two young love birds married and settled in Oregon, where Mom was from. In less than a decade, they were a bustling family of five.

Enabling Mom to stay home to raise us kids required immense sacrifice from both of my parents. While most of their peers were buying new homes and new cars, my folks rented modest homes and relied on an older model station wagon for transportation. In addition to his more than full-time career position with the finance division of General Motors called GMAC, Dad also worked a second and sometimes even a third job to make ends meet. His work demands notwithstanding, my dad was tireless and always seemed to "be there" whenever I needed him.

When I started playing Little League baseball at the age of eight, my dad volunteered to be the team coach (a position he served in for five years). Whenever I had a question he was always quick to provide wise counsel. I remember asking him at breakfast one morning how I could learn about pro baseball. He set his newspaper down and thoughtfully rubbed his chin for a moment. Then, as if he had invented the game himself, he delivered sage advice, "Buzz" (my nickname as a boy), he said, "I would suggest you set your sights a bit lower at first and start by just learning about a single player. When you know everything about that player, then you can learn about the teammates he plays next to, and then about his team, and then about their division, and then about their league, and then about the other league, and then about the playoffs and then about the World Series." He showed me how to read a box score on the sports page, how to calculate a batting average, how to follow the standings and explained what a pennant race was.

A week later I asked "who" I should learn about in order to commence my formal pro baseball education. Again he pondered my inquiry (his dramatic effect, whether intentional or not, seared into my consciousness forever). Opening that morning's newspaper, he announced, "Well, here's a fellow I actually happen to know. He's from Sacramento, and his team is close by. His name is Rick Monday. He plays centerfield for the Oakland Athletics." And just like that, my decades-long allegiance to the Oakland A's began.

I lived and breathed baseball for the next several years of boyhood. When not playing the game myself, I would lay out in the yard under the magnificent oak tree that towered over our house and listen to the play-by-play of A's baseball on my own personal nine-volt transistor radio. I was able to own such a treasure because I put into practice at an early age the work ethic I saw and admired in my dad. In addition to doing my household chores for a small weekly allowance, I made money collecting empty pop bottles around the neighborhood and hauling them in a wagon to the local grocery store for their redemption value. I also earned a fair amount cleaning up after that aforementioned oak tree, which, each fall, produced an infinite number of leaves to be raked. I got my first "real" job at age 14, busing tables at the Sizzler Steakhouse down the road. In addition to my $1.65 per hour wage, I collected meat scraps and sold them for a dollar a bag to customers with dogs at home.

But, like my dad, in addition to working hard, I also sought to learn and put into practice the virtues of contentment and balance. In addition to baseball and work, I also applied myself diligently at school. Dad always spoke highly of education and lamented the fact that he never finished college. I learned to play piano and discovered the beauty of music, and I became immersed in the secret realm of imagination that exists in reading.

Almost daily during the hot doldrums of summer, I would ride my proudly purchased second-hand purple Stingray bike three miles to the local library and hole-up in a corner underneath the air conditioning fan to read the tales of "Lad: A Dog" by Albert Peyson Terhune. I loved the idea of having a dog and spent many hours dreaming about frolicking with a collie dog like Lad at the Terhune's New Jersey estate, called "SunnyBank". Sadly, my dad had been attacked by a dog as a boy and so never liked them much and despite my incessant pleas, he never allowed me to have a dog. My mom later told me that I ruined many Christmases for my folks when, at the end of opening all the presents under the tree, they would see the profound disappointment on my face when my last package did not contain that dreamed-of note that I hoped would say, "Go look in the garage for your new puppy." But even through my disappointments I learned to respect my dad's decisions as he led his family through the trials and challenges of life.

I also learned, with a little help from my dad, to respect my mother. Like all teenage boys, I grew restless with my mother's ever-present shadow and what I deemed to be her severe over-protectiveness. Not appreciating the incredible gift of a mom at home, I longed for the freedom I thought my friends enjoyed because their moms worked away from the home. One day my teenage impetuousness came to a head, and I raised my voice to challenge my mother's authority. I was quite a bit bigger physically than she was and for the first time I sensed a bit of cowering in her voice as she tried to stand her ground. The issue was really quite mundane. I was clearly in need of a haircut but simply didn't want to be bothered with it. So I launched into a diatribe about becoming a man, and my independence, and my right to self-determination, blah, blah, blah. I think I even argued that I should have long hair because Jesus had long hair. Suffice it to say, I was totally out of line and for no legitimate reason.

When my dad learned about my escapade that evening after dinner, he confronted me head on. Having been emboldened by my perceived victory over Mom earlier in the day, I was momentarily blinded to reality. The argument with Dad lasted less than a minute. He was furious about how I had treated Mom and then, when I attempted to challenge him, I found myself quickly and expertly pinned to the hallway wall, toes barely touching the ground. With a guttural grizzly-like growl my father told me that I could take a run at him anytime I thought I might be ready, but if I ever verbally threatened my mother again, it might well be the last thing I ever did. My bravado fled immediately, and I meekly nodded assent. I didn't even attempt to rebut his contention that I was verbally abusive to Mom because even though I hadn't been, I could understand how she might have seen it that way. Respect was a hard-learned lesson, but one I never forgot. I learned scores of such life lessons from my dad that molded my understanding of fatherhood. In his own way, I think he even modeled for me rudimentary concepts of grace and forgiveness, though he would not become personally familiar with them, from a Biblical perspective, until later in his life.

In addition to being blessed with a temporal fatherly role model, I also learned about being a man, husband and dad from my Heavenly Father. Principal among those lessons was the truth that being a good husband precedes being a good father. Showing your children that you love them by the example of first loving and caring for their mother is one of the greatest gifts a father can bestow upon his kids. And, in so doing, you establish an environment of safety, security and confidence where young ones can grow strong physically, emotionally and spiritually.

One of the tough lessons I learned as a dad, was the fact that your children can (and often will) imitate your bad traits as well as your good ones. I tend to be a rather driven person, and striving for perfection (or at least to be the best I can be) was something I seemed to do from early on. Whether it was school or baseball or even washing dishes (I got promoted from busboy), I always tried my best. I can still hear my dad pontificate, "If it's worth doing at all, it's worth doing right." In many respects, it was a good mantra to live by, and I succeeded in many aspects of life by applying it (e.g., college, law school, law firm partnership, etc.). At the same time, however, I also learned valuable lessons from failure. Well, maybe not failure exactly, but missing the mark I'd set for myself ... coming in second. Prime examples of this for me came repeatedly in the realm of sports.

Maybe I was just a "want-to-be" jock, but sports played a huge role in my formative years. In ninth grade, I was a very small kid because I was actually a year younger than most of my peers. (Starting school at the age of four because I was academically ready cost me dearly growing up in sports.) Though I wrestled at the fly-weight, 105-pound class, what I really wanted to do was play basketball because that's where the glory was (and, in turn, the girls). Due to my size, the only chance I had to make the team was to out-hustle everyone else because I certainly couldn't rebound, let alone shoot, over most of the other players. More than 100 boys tried out for the ninth-grade squad, and weekly roster cuts of 20 to 25 were made over a grueling month-long tryout period. At the last session of tryouts before the season started, the coach announced he would be carrying 15 kids on the team. At that point there were only 16 of us left on the tryout roster. When the final roster was posted the next day, I wasn't on it. High school football was also out of the question for me because some of the kids were nearly double my size, and, by that time I was working three shifts a week as an apprentice assistant-cook (another Sizzler promotion). So, once again, I focused my attention on baseball.

Playing ball through Little League and then Babe Ruth League, I developed into a pretty good first baseman (as a lefty), a decent pitcher (because lefty's have a natural curve ball) and a reliable base hitter (not much in the long-ball department but a consistent batting average over .400). Yet, each year, for three consecutive years, when it came time to name the league's all-star team that would represent our town in tournaments throughout the summer, I was named as an "alternate". The most painful aspect of this, besides the humiliation of missing the mark three years in a row, was that I found myself hoping one of my friends would get injured so I would be called up to the team. How pathetic is that?

The high school varsity baseball squad never materialized for me either because there was a giant 6'4" left-handed superstar first baseman. He was also captain of the football team and the basketball team and a year ahead of me in school. He would never relinquish the first-base bag to pint-sized me until he graduated (and, of course, I got hauled off to Montana when my senior year finally arrived). Even my alternate spring sport of tennis was a frustration. I played steadily and victoriously on the number one doubles team but was never quite able to break into the singles circuit. As the old Avis Rental Car slogan used to suggest, when you're only second best you've just got to try harder. And I did, and I succeeded in many endeavors. But, as a dad, I saw that drive to try harder and strive for success become a potential demon in my house.

Like her father, Noelle was a first born. I poured everything into that little girl. She was (and is) my pride and joy. And, like her father, she too began imitating her dad's traits early on. One Saturday after lunch, kindergartner Noelle set out to do her "homework" ... a two sentence story about her day coupled with a drawing. When I heard a faint pound on the table coupled with a whimper, I came into the kitchen where she was working and witnessed Noelle crunching up a piece of paper and throwing it into the corner on top of several other similarly discarded drawing attempts. "I just can't draw this right," Noelle exclaimed in an exasperated tone unbecoming my tender 5-year-old girl. I tried, in my most understanding dad voice, to console her,

"That's okay, honey, you don't have to draw it perfectly." "Oh yes I do!" she snapped back. Suddenly, I realized this wasn't really about Noelle's drawing at all, this was about me. I had inadvertently and unknowingly imposed my own driven nature onto my precious little girl. I was ruining my child. I was failing as her father. Of course, I didn't confess this to Noelle, and she got past her frustration in less than a minute and was off to play, but I was devastated for weeks. I resolved right then and there to ease up on myself and to hopefully thereby teach my children the joy of exploration without the self-imposed pressure of a perfect performance every time.

Another dad lesson I learned the hard way came again in the context of baseball (I just don't know what it is about that sport and my life lessons). I will always cherish my memory of the first Oakland A's game my dad took me to as a boy. He came home from work early to pick me up, and we drove to Oakland. It was just the two of us talking about baseball and life. We had hot chocolate in an old thermos and pre-cooked hot dogs wrapped in tin foil to keep them warm. Dad bought a bag of salted peanuts in the shell from a stadium barker, and as we ate them we laughed and threw the shells on the stadium floor where they crunched loudly when I'd step on them. The A's took an early lead as a waning moon rose slowly over the stadium's centerfield wall. When we opened the hot dogs for dinner during the bottom of the fourth inning, they were still piping hot. The steam and aroma rose gloriously into the crisp evening air as we bit into the soggy bun filled with mustard, relish, and the Oscar Meyer delicacy. After the game, on our way out of the stadium, Dad bought me an A's team pennant. It was a perfect night. I wanted to create a similar special memory for Noelle.

At the time I was coaching Noelle's Pony League softball team called the Mermaids (only in Pacific Grove would a team have such a name). Just as I had done that first year out of college, I teamed up with a buddy to coach, only this time I had a child on the squad. Our team wasn't the most competitive in the league because we had taken a different tack during the pre-season draft. First off, I found it a bit odd to be "drafting" little 10- and 11-year old girls for a team, but I digress. Our plan was not to create a winning team in the conventional baseball sense, but rather to surround our girls with good kids and good families with the hope of facilitating a positive peer group for them. Now, I know some might think that was a bit manipulative on my part, and they would be correct. I believe it is part of a dad's job to control, maneuver, sway, help, inspire, cajole, direct and in all other manner gently manipulate his kids toward healthy choices. I coached all three of my children for the same two-year span (ages 10 to 11) and to this day think it was one of my most rewarding experiences as a dad.

So, I planned a daddy-daughter date with Noelle to go to an A's game. I carefully set it all up to mirror that fond memory I had with my dad, including the hot chocolate and the mushy hot dogs. We talked about it and planned together for weeks. Finally the big day arrived, but wouldn't you know it, a client had an 11th-hour emergency that caused me to be late getting home. I was frustrated and angry with myself because I so wanted Noelle to experience the thrill of pre-game batting practice, the anticipation of possibly getting a foul ball hit our way (we both brought our ball gloves to catch such an errant treasure), the national anthem, the umpire yelling "play ball!" and the crowd roaring as the first pitch was delivered ... for a called strike! But all that was in jeopardy because I had elected to take that last client call.

So, I was in turbo mode as I flew into the house. Noelle was dutifully waiting for me, sitting patiently on the couch, already packed and brimming with excitement. Lorrie had our dinner and a variety of snacks ready to go in a back pack (though she never fully understood my insistence on the soggy hot dogs). All I had to do was change clothes. I did so in a flash, and we were off. I was still tense from my work delay, and Noelle could sense it so she sat quietly in the passenger seat while my mind raced to calculate the mileage and estimate whether we would arrive in time for the first pitch. It would be close, very close, but with light traffic and a little luck, we might just make it in time.

Then, less than a mile from the house I started doing what I always hated my parents doing - going through the trip checklist after you've already left on the trip. Noelle was a good helper. "Check, check, check," she said as I went through my mental list until I asked about her coat. "Uh, oh," she said, "I think I left it on the couch. I'm sorry Daddy." "You what?!" My frustration with myself and my client and with the potential of being late to the game boiled over, and I unfairly lashed out at Noelle. Knowing it would get cold at the ballgame, I whipped the car around and raced back to the house. I slammed the car door as I stormed up to the house to fetch the neglected jacket. I then gruffly re-entered the car and started off again. The whole incident couldn't have taken more than five minutes, but I proceeded nonetheless to lecture Noelle on the need to be more responsible. She just sat there mute and received the brunt of my wrath without defense. A few miles later I realized how ridiculous I had been, and I apologized. Noelle, in a display of far greater maturity than her father had been exhibiting, graciously forgave me, and we went on to enjoy a wonderful evening at the Oakland Coliseum.

A few years later, as I was extolling the benefits of daddy-daughter dates and recalling my ballgame date with Noelle to a friend, Noelle stepped into the room. I asked if she remembered our epic date that night. Without hesitation she said, " Oh yes, Dad, I remember. That was the time you yelled at me for forgetting my coat." I was crushed to discover that the perfect evening I had engendered in my memory had never registered with Noelle. All she remembered was my horrible moment of parental failure. Ouch! Fathers beware ... you never know what kind of indelible impression you may be making on your children.

Another baseball-related story comes to mind as I write this. For Father's Day each year, in response to the inevitable and expected question, "What do you want to do on your special day, Daddy?" I decided to turn the tables. I created the tradition of answering that question, "I want to do whatever YOU want to do ... as long as I get to do it with YOU." The kids loved this response, and it was easy to accommodate all three of them when they were little because their idea of a fun activity was simple, such as going to the beach, making s'mores, or going to the ice cream shop. I loved this approach to Father's Day because it really was my heart's desire to spend time with my family. Many dads I know seek personal away time on their special day (e.g., playing golf or knocking off some extravagant bucket-list item), but not me. My "hobby" had become my family, and that is where I wanted to spend my time. Years later, when facing the prospect of fatherhood, my son-in-law, Jeff, would ask me how much time he should plan for himself once the baby arrived. My answer was simple and immediate. "Zero," I said. I think he was both shocked and disappointed, hoping I might allow for at least 10 percent. I explained that zero was not really as difficult as it may sound because my self-interests dissipated when I had children. Zero was actually quite easy because in reality it was 100 percent for me. Time spent with my kids was time spent on myself.

As the kids grew older, however, it became increasingly difficult to accommodate all three of them on Father's Day because their proposed activities became more complex and time-consuming. Not that I didn't want to do them all, but there are only so many hours in a day. So, we would sit around the breakfast table before church and decide what everyone would enjoy doing together. One year the family choice was to go to a baseball game. Of course, that was an easy yes for me, and I looked in the newspaper to see if the Oakland A's were in town. Sadly, they were on the road that weekend, but the other nearby team, the San Francisco Giants, were playing at home.

The Giants were having a good year, and that day they were playing the Chicago Cubs. The Cubs' big stick was a fellow named Sammy Sosa. He and former Oakland A's star, Mark McGuire, were locked in a historic home-run record chase. When I called the ball park to ask if there were any tickets available, I was told the game was sold out but that they always reserved 200 bleacher seat tickets for last-minute fans. The voice on the phone said there was a special ticket kiosk in the back parking lot behind left field and that they sold the tickets there first come-first served. We decided to take a chance on getting six tickets (a friend of ours from college days, from Chicago no less, happened to be visiting us at the time). We all agreed that if we couldn't get into the game, we'd just go explore San Francisco for the day instead.

We went to the early Sunday service and left for the stadium directly from church. It would be nip and tuck regarding the timing of everything but it was, after all, an adventure and everyone was game for fun in whatever form it might take. Surprisingly, we were among the fortunate few to get the last-minute back-of-the-bleacher tickets that day. As we came into the stadium from behind the left field bleachers, I could hear the crack of batting practice bats smacking the ball around. We couldn't see anything from down below and behind the towering bleachers ahead of us, but I squeezed Grant's hand and said, "Wouldn't it be cool if we got to see Sammy Sosa take batting practice? Maybe he would hit one our way since we are out in the bleachers." Without a word Grant grabbed his ball-glove from my backpack and began running toward the back side of the bleachers, "Come on dad, and hurry up!" Lorrie smiled and nodded that I should go on ahead of her to appease Grant (and myself, of course). I blew her a quick kiss and ran after my son.

Now, you may not believe this, but what happened next is absolutely true. As we came out of the entrance tunnel and into the daylight, I caught up with Grant. We were scouring the scene looking for the quickest way to access the mountainous bleachers in front of us. Then, someone in the distance yelled to friend, "Look! He's coming to the plate ... Sammy Sosa is up!" Grant could barely contain himself and grabbed my hand to pull me along faster. Just then, we heard the crisp crack of a bat. We looked up into the noon day sun and saw the heads of those sitting at the top of the bleacher seats look up as if following a baseball in the sky. A sea of gloved hands went up in unison and then the object of everyone's attention appeared, soaring high in the sky and ... over the bleachers.

The Sammy Sosa home run ball landed on the pavement behind the bleachers and only 20 feet in front of us. It bounced high and careened to my left. I momentarily lost my senses and let go of Grant's hand to chase after the ball. After a five-second scurry, I grabbed it and, at the same time, about seven other people, mostly kids, grabbed me. It was a mad scrum for the coveted baseball. I dropped to one knee and then went into the fetal position to protect my prize. I was punched, pinched, kicked and slapped (all in good fun I'm sure) but held on tightly to the treasure. Eventually I made it back to my feet and emerged, baseball firmly in my grip, and raised my hand in victory! I ran over to a somewhat stunned but smiling Grant and proudly placed the ball in his gloved hand and announced, "Happy Father's Day, Grant!"

Even on non-holiday weekends I sought out time with my kids. Since Saturdays were often occupied with Pony League softball and baseball and the never-ending "chore" list, Sunday became the natural day for us to do special family things together. I dubbed these times "Sunday Adventures". We seldom did anything extraordinary, but we had a knack for making the everyday seem exceptional. We would often go exploring along the coast or in the nearby Del Monte Forest. I learned, however, to check my exuberance for adventure and my penchant for going "off trail" because sometimes the kids couldn't keep up. We climbed Signal Hill, picked huckleberries, wandered along seldom used forest trails, discovered Indian Village, explored secret beaches and coves and went on bike rides. Though our destination was always a surprise to the kids, the end of each Sunday Adventure was not. Our tradition was perhaps mundane but nonetheless beloved by our kids. After returning home and washing up, we always prepared a special Sunday dinner often consisting of corned beef hash and eggs (with some green pepper, tomato, and a little cheddar cheese sprinkled on top). Then we'd all get into our "happy pants" (a.k.a. pajamas) and set up TV trays in the family room. When all were seated and after a thankful prayer for the day we had enjoyed together, we'd settle in to dine while watching "Dr. Quinn - Medicine Woman". I know, I know ... weird, but it worked for us and will always be a cherished memory of family tradition.

Speaking of traditions, we had a lot of them. I'm not sure what the attraction was, maybe the comfort of the known and regular, but we created oodles of traditions. We even joked that creating new traditions was a kind of tradition itself. Some of our traditions revolved around the Christmas season. Of course, there were always the Christmas programs at school, the chorus performances at the downtown tree lighting and the mall, and the seemingly never ending middle school band recitals, but we created some unique "Bridges" family traditions as well. Several hearkened back to traditions my dad instituted when I was a boy.

We didn't have much money when I was growing up, so we hardly ever went out to eat. Once in a blue moon we might go to Sambo's for a Sunday brunch, but very seldom did we go out for dinner. Christmas Eve, however, was special and we knew we were in for an outing. Burgers! We always went to a local restaurant (usually Denny's or Sizzler) and had burgers and fries before driving around the neighborhoods to look at Christmas lights. So, to keep a good thing going, I instituted the same program for my family only we worked Christmas Eve church service into the mix and added milk shakes to the menu.

Another tradition my dad kind of inadvertently initiated for me had to do with Rudolph the Red-Nosed Reindeer. I have always been a huge fan of the Claymation cartoon narrated by Burl Ives. During my boyhood, it was "the" pre-Christmas day highlight of every Christmas season for me. I memorized every word to every song in the show as well as much of the dialogue. One of my favorite lines was when the young doe Clarice flirtingly tells Rudolf what she thinks of his red nose, and, in response, the young buck takes off flying and exclaims to the world, "I'm cute! I'm cute! I'm CUTE!" Everything about that show was pure magic, and to this day I am careful not to miss it.

The Rudolph tradition began the December following my fifth birthday. We lived in Reno, Nevada, at the time and were going to my grandparents' house in Portland, Oregon, for Christmas. My mom was six months pregnant with my little brother so she and my three-year-old sister Robin took a plane. We couldn't afford four plane tickets, and my dad had to work right up to the day of Christmas Eve anyway, so I was assigned to keep him company during the long drive north. We left early in the morning, just me and my dad. The weather was rough, and we hit snow as we headed over the Sierras, but the roads were plowed so it wasn't much of an issue. We crossed through northern California and then finally into Oregon.

At around 3 p.m. we approached the mountainous area call Grant's Pass. The snow was falling hard, and the highway patrol was pulling vehicles over to advise that tire chains were required in order to traverse the mountain. My dad was an expert with tire chains and, being always prepared, he had a set in the trunk. But even with chains, the officer still discouraged travel because the roads were icy and treacherous. My dad was intimately familiar with this pass having driven it scores of times during his previous years in Oregon spent "chasing skips" (repossessing cars; Dad's first job for General Motors). Because it was important that we join the family for Christmas, Dad decided to proceed over the pass despite the warnings.

As we headed up the mountain, the wind whipped and the snow fell, even harder. Not only was the road slick, but visibility was near zero in the blizzard-like conditions. My dad didn't seem worried, but I knew it was serious when he reached over to put his hand on my shoulder and said, "Buzz, I'm going to need to really concentrate on my driving for the next hour, so I need you to sit real still and be quiet. Can you do that for me, partner?" Of course I chimed in with a ready, "Yes sir!" I was impressed with my dad's caution and skill as he crawled up and over the pass that day.

When we got to the other side of the mountain the snowfall lightened and the tension in the car dissipated. Dad visibly relaxed and started up a conversation with me. We had survived the ordeal and would be in Portland in a few short hours. At the next small town we came to, Dad pulled into a gas station to fill up and buy some snacks for us. When he came back to the car, he presented me with a special prize for having been so helpful during the drive. It was an inflatable Rudolph!

I wasn't familiar with the story, so Dad told it to me as we drove north. I loved that inflatable Rudolph, and it became one of my favorite Christmas toys. Each succeeding year we would inflate it and place it near the Christmas tree. The next year when I discovered the animated television program about my favorite reindeer, I couldn't be happier. Many years later, when Dad was in his 70s, he and Mom were scheduled to visit us in Pacific Grove for the holiday. I found an identical Rudolph toy and gave it to my dad for Christmas. We laughed together as we recounted (for the umpteenth time) our sojourn over Grant's Pass so long ago. Dad decided to leave the toy with us to become a part of our annual Christmas decorations. Dad's great-grandchildren now enjoy Rudolph, too!

Back in the day, the Christmas Eve service at Calvary Chapel was extremely family-oriented. It usually included a short Bible message, a reading from Luke's gospel and then special music performances presented by members of the congregation. It was kind of like an old fashion sing-around-the-piano family time, very low-key and fun. Since Lorrie and I were on the worship team, we were asked one year if our family might do a number together. It sounded like fun, and we assumed the kids would enjoy the experience. As the years passed, our Christmas offerings became a mainstay at the annual event and we affectionately became known as the Bridges-von Trapp family (a more-than-kind reference to the "Sound of Music" family). Sometimes we would expand the ensemble to include our entire Bible study group. Over the years we performed many types of music and included sign language, flute solos by the girls, theatrical components, contemporary remakes of old carols, and once, a complex 4-part harmony rendition of an old Southern spiritual. The funny thing is that, as much as I thought the kids reveled in these performances, I found out years later they were happiest when we stopped doing them.

During one Christmas Eve burger dinner when the kids were home from college, I mused aloud about the good old days and how fun it had been to sing as a family. To my utter surprise, each of the kids said how glad they were when they finally didn't have to do that anymore. What? "Have" to do that anymore? Unbeknownst to me, the pressure of performing on Christmas Eve had become a burden on the kids and they couldn't wait for it to be over, so "Christmas fun could finally begin." Hmmm, an important lesson there: always check in with the kids to see if what you think is fun is as fun for the kids. Unfortunately for my kids, I learned that lesson a bit late, but we all laugh about it now, and my kids assure me they learned volumes from my parenting miscues.

I also found a way to apply one of my other loves in life, music, to fatherhood. When each of the kids was born, I wrote them a song to be sung at their baby dedication. I printed and framed the lyrics and gave them copies when they got older. Of course, in addition to the enjoyment of writing the songs, I had an ulterior motive. I wanted to impart to them the importance of Christ and our prayers that they would submit to His Lordship in their lives. Because I had also written a song for Lorrie when we got married (which I sang to her during our ceremony), I thought it appropriate to write songs for the kids when they got married as well. Yet another opportunity, I thought, to speak into their lives through music in a way I hoped would be long-lasting.

Noelle was our first to get married. The person she chose was a God-loving young man named Chris, who was studying to become a pastor. They met during their junior year in college (though they went to different Christian universities in Southern California). When it came time for Chris to "pop the question", he wanted to do so during sunset on the beach in Carmel. He painstakingly made all the arrangements for his proposal. Being an honorable sort, Chris wanted to ask me for Noelle's hand before asking her. The problem was he hadn't figured I'd be so hard to get alone. Chris devised a plan to invite me out for an early morning run on the beach the day before his proposal date with Noelle. I was certainly game for a run but also insisted that Noelle come along with us. "Come on, it will be fun, just the three of us!" Chris was out of options. He couldn't very well ask me for Noelle's hand with her standing there. So, Chris conspired with Lorrie, and the two of them came up with a Plan B.

That evening, as I was getting into bed (in my pajamas nonetheless), Chris knocked on our bedroom door. Lorrie, knowing what was about to transpire, invited him in. Now, I thought this was a bit forward, not to mention awkward, for the boyfriend to invite himself into my bedroom when I was nodding off for the night. But not just into my bedroom - onto my bed. Chris hopped right up on the end of the bed. Startled, I sat up and looked at him. "John," he said, "we need to talk." The pre-sleep cloud swirling in my mind quickly vanished as I realized what was happening. I looked helplessly over at Lorrie, and she was grinning from ear-to-ear. I was trapped. Of course, I didn't really mind all that much because I knew Noelle had fallen deeply in love with this young man and that he would selflessly cherish and care for her forever.

Chris's planning and intention to make his engagement proposal unique and special also blessed me as I recalled my utter failure to do the same. I just don't know if I'll ever recover from my hurried driveway proposal and be able to make it up to my lovely Lorraine. The proposals of our other two children were equally memorable. Maybe the ineptness of my story sank deep into their collective consciences as something to be avoided. Jeff proposed to Whitney on a coastal bluff in Laguna Beach. Jeff is an accomplished artist, and he was painting a picture of a young couple watching a romantic sunset. When Whitney "happened" by (it was all pre-planned of course), Jeff knelt and asked if he could "paint her into the rest of his life." Grant surprised Taylor in December beneath a 50-foot-tall Christmas tree displayed in the middle of Union Square in San Francisco while both families and many friends watched from a fourth-story window in the Macy's building across the street. All three engagements were pure magic!

After Noelle's engagement, I began praying about the wedding song I would write for the two of them. For me, writing songs has always been more about listening than speaking. I have no particular training in writing songs but always just listened for the music and lyrics to come from God. I see myself as more of a conduit for God to communicate through song than for me to do so myself. The lyrics to Noelle's wedding song came to me almost instantly the first time I sat down to "listen" for them, but oddly, the music did not follow. This had never happened to me before. In the past, the music and lyrics always seemed to come concurrently, kind of just organically happening. I was puzzled. For weeks I waited and listened ... but nothing. Then I sat down and purposed to write music to fit with the lyrics ... but nothing. Confused and frustrated, I decided to set the whole idea aside. Maybe I wasn't supposed to write wedding songs for my kids. Maybe that was reserved only for Lorrie.

A few weeks later, during an early morning run along the coast, I began singing Noelle's baby dedication song and reminiscing about all the wonderful times we had experienced growing up together. Then, almost like a flash of lightning, it came to me. The music for the Noelle's wedding song lyrics had been right there in front of me the whole time. I had already written it ... 23 years earlier. I began to sing the wedding lyrics to the baby dedication music, and the two fit hand in glove. The revelation shook me to the core, and I was elated to the point of tears. I eventually wrote wedding songs in a similar fashion for Whitney and Grant, using their baby song music. Today I am continuing the tradition by writing baby dedication songs for each of my grandchildren: for Colton Sterling ("The Namesake"), for Hayley Grace ("A Kiss Blown by God"), for Andrew John ("Overjoyed") and for Mackenzie Jane ("Thousand Prayers"). As great as being a Dad was and is, being a Granddad is sometimes even better.

Another tradition inspired by my parents took an interesting turn when applied to my family. When I married Lorrie, my folks accepted her into our family so completely that she received the moniker, "number 4" ... as in "the fourth child". In turn, my brother-in-law, Greg, became number 5 and my sister-in-law, Laura, number 6. The unconditional love and acceptance extended by my parents to the spouses of their children was as inspiring to me as it was a blessing. As our children married we conferred the same numeric status on their spouses except in the case of Grant's wife, Taylor. She received an early label.

Noelle and Chris lived in Portland, Oregon, for two years while Chris was in seminary. For Easter one year, Lorrie and I drove up the coast to see them. We visited six lighthouses on the way including Heceta Head which is the most famous tower on the Oregon coast. Joining us in the Ritter's small apartment for the holiday weekend were Grant and his girlfriend Taylor. Grant and Taylor were serious about each other but no formal announcement had yet been made about an engagement. We all liked Taylor a lot and Lorrie even admonished Grant (with a motherly wink) that he'd better not let her get away.

During the family banter that took place while we all enjoyed the spectacular Easter meal Noelle had prepared, I affectionately referred to Chris as our "number 4". The conversation then shifted to the story of how Lorrie was also a "number 4" and the tradition my parents had established. After a few minutes of storytelling revolving around this topic, I realized Taylor might be feeling a bit awkward because she had no status in the family let alone a numeric moniker. I stopped the conversation and took Taylor by the hand, and with just a hint of playful drama, I looked deep into her wonderfully beautiful brown eyes and asked, "Tay, I just realized you don't have a number, and that is probably awkward. I'm sorry. How should we refer to you?" Always quick on her feet and ready, willing and quite able to engage in family shenanigans, Taylor demurely said she'd like to think about it for a few minutes. I said, "Okay by me, you can have five." Five more minutes of rich family conversation ensued before I once again posed the question to Taylor. Her answer brought a tear to my eye and by it I knew instantly that this was a very special girl indeed, and that Grant should definitely not let her get away. In her sweetly confident way, and with a twinkle of fun in her eye, Taylor now took my hand and said, "John, I've thought about your question and think I'd like to be called: 5/6ths." Intrigued, I inquired a bit further, "Why 5/6ths, Taylor?" She explained, "Well, you know that Grant and I love each other, and I hope to someday become number 6 in this family, but until that day I think I would be most comfortable with 5/6ths. You see, I want to leave room for Jesus to make the final decision." My heart melted, and I couldn't wait for her to become our full-fledged "number 6". Many months later at their wedding Chris performed the ceremony, and after the vows and kiss he proudly introduced his new sister-in-law, Taylor, to the assembled family and friends as, "a whole 6."

Looking back, it seems easier to identify the things I did wrong as a father than it is to define what I did right. Sometimes I think it was only by God's grace that my children survived my foibles. Four things I do, however, believe I (actually "we" ... truth be known Lorrie deserves more credit than I do) did right revolved around making the presence of God known in our home.

As mentioned several times, Lorrie and I have always hosted a weekly Bible study at our house. It started in college, even before we were married, and continued more-or-less consistently throughout our early work years, law school years and then as we settled in Pacific Grove. As important as the fellowship and teaching were to us, I think the mere fact that it "happened" in our home each week made a serious impression on our kids. Of course, when they were little, they didn't actually participate. And as they grew older, they were invited but not expected, to join in. Just the regularity of reading the Bible and praying and singing worship songs in our home spoke volumes to little ears. As the Bible study couples became families, all were invited to bring their children. I can't begin to count the number of small children who, at our house, first learned to sleep away from the comfort of their own crib or bed. We had some unruly moments to be sure, but we all just kind of flowed with it.

When our kids got older, while our Bible study met in the living room, they began holding "kid's Bible club" for the younger ones in the back family room. They modeled this time after the AWANA program they enjoyed on

Wednesday nights. AWANA was a second thing I think we did right. AWANA (Approved Workmen Are Not Ashamed) is a weekly youth group/Bible club (kind of like Scouts) for children ages 4 to 14. Our church didn't have such a program, so we joined one at a small Baptist church in Monterey. The kids loved the Bible memory exercises and the games and snacks and fun times. Twice a year they participated in AWANA "Olympics" held in a gym in Salinas where clubs from around the county competed in sporting-type events (such as three-legged racing and balloon popping) for prizes. This activity was a particular favorite of young Grant who was a "busy" boy and somewhat less interested in the memorization work.

Lorrie and I adopted a unique approach to the AWANA club time. Different from any other church-related activity we had ever been involved with, for once, we decided not to volunteer to help. Admittedly, this atypical behavior made us feel a bit guilty, but we chose nonetheless to redeem the two hours each Wednesday night by using the time as our "date night". In the busyness and frazzle of our lives during that season, it was nearly impossible to find any quality time to focus on each other … and, as I said, being a good husband is a key to being a good dad. So, each Wednesday, after dropping the kids off at AWANA (which for us was easy as they would literally run from the car into the church in anticipation of club time with their friends), Lorrie and I would stroll the streets of Monterey and explore the many funky and often exotic little hole-in-the-wall restaurants along Lighthouse Avenue.

Because I was a standard meat and potatoes guy, many of the cuisine offerings along Lighthouse were foreign to me. Monterey is known as the language capitol of the world thanks to the influences of the Defense Language Institute and Middlebury Institute of International Studies which attract people from all over the world. Consequently, the variety of eateries is almost endless. Lorrie is much more of a foodie than I am, so she was always encouraging me to try something "different". In an effort to bless my wife, I would reluctantly allow myself to be dragged into very strange places. One evening in particular I'll never forget.

The place was called Tabouli's. Tabouli is a type of salad served in the Middle East. This restaurant was run by one man, just one. He was the owner, manager, host, waiter, cashier, cook, dishwasher and busboy. When he had to go to the bank or run some other errand in the middle of the day, he would put a simple sign in the window that read, "Be back soon." When he went home to Lebanon to visit family for a month or more at a time, he'd put the same simple sign in the window that read, "Be back soon." It was an odd way to run a business, but he seemed to thrive.

Lorrie had clipped a two-for-one coupon and insisted we try it out. As we opened the door, I was greeted with a completely foreign world. The music was Middle Eastern as was the furniture. The posters on the wall were of Istanbul and Kuwait and Egypt. The smells were intriguing and frightening at the same time. Most of the people looked like they were from elsewhere, and the only word I recognized on the elaborate wall menu was chicken. I started backing out of the door almost before taking the first step inside. Lorrie laughed and pulled me in. The owner saw my hesitancy and with a big smile beckoned to me in a warm friendly voice, "Come, come taste. You'll like!" So I did. And

I did! It has since become one of our favorite spots for a quick bite.

A third thing I believe we did right related to music. As you know by now, music has and always will be a powerful force in my life. The decade of the 1970s was a great period for music, and to this day I can still sing many of the songs that were indelibly grafted into my mind and heart during my teenage years. Being a hopeless romantic, some of my favorite artists included the likes of Dan Fogelberg, Jim Croce and David Gates. The kids laugh at Lorrie and I when sometimes an old tune comes on the radio and we'll stop everything, and have a "moment" together, singing and remembering. I actually told Lorrie I first loved her by singing to her the Jim Croce song, "So I'll Have to say I Love You in a Song". Like I said, I'm hopeless. Well, knowing the incredible impact music had on my life as a young person, I purposed to ensure the music my children listened to would be edifying and Christ-focused.

Fortunately for our family, the national Christian radio station K-LOVE came on the air about the time our kids became interested in music. For almost two decades, very little music was played in our home, or in our car, that was not "CCM", Contemporary Christian Music. We were huge fans and supporters of CCM, and as a family embraced it to the maximum. We sought out concerts by CCM artists and took the kids as often as we could. We bought CDs and posters. Everything every teenager loves about "their" music, we embraced together as a family ... in the genre of CCM.

I'll never forget taking Noelle to her first concert. The other two children were too young to be "into" music yet, but Noelle was right at that age when music was beginning to matter. We went to a concert in San Jose featuring a female artist whose music and lyrics spoke passionately about Christ and issues faced by girls and young women. Her name was Margaret Becker, affectionately known in our house as Maggie. At the end of the show she sang her most popular song at the time, which Noelle knew by heart thanks to K-LOVE. The audience was emotionally moved and a spontaneous standing ovation ensued as Maggie and her band left the stage. Noelle looked up at me and asked why everyone was standing. I told her it was to show their appreciation for the wonderful concert and to try to coax the artist back to the stage for more. When Noelle heard this she leapt up, stood on her tiptoes and clapped wildly. As a soft chant for an encore began circulating through the room, Noelle looked up and asked me what an encore was. As I was explaining it to her over the clamor of the crowd, Becker and her band slowly returned to the stage and the lights once again came up. With a face beaming with innocence and delight, Noelle squeezed my hand tight and said in a hushed tone, "Daddy it worked … it really worked!"

Many concerts and many blessings followed that night. We saw dozens of CCM artists and for each concert we went to, the kids' t-shirt, wall-poster and CD collections grew. We were more than happy to "spoil" them with these trinkets as we knew how well a devotion to Christian music would serve them as they grew up in a world full of if desirable influences and temptations. Needless to say, MTV was never watched at our house.

As all of our kids became full-fledged teenagers, another amazing musical blessing happened. A young CCM promoter decided to host a festival in Monterey, called Spirit West

Coast. Coincidentally, Lorrie and I led a small worship team at the first organizational meeting the local community had with this promoter. I guess you could say we were supporters of the festival from its inception. The event spanned three days in late July. There were six different stages and more than 30 artists and speakers. It was an absolutely amazing opportunity for us to further encourage our kids about the values and virtues of Christian music.

That first year (and there would be many festivals to follow that we attended), we wanted to get good seats on the main stage lawn. It was first-come first-served and very casual. You just put down your blanket and a cooler, and you had the spot for the day. We were on the lawn at sunrise all three days and scored marvelous seats directly behind the front-row section that was set aside for premium ticket holders. When the big names sang in the late afternoon and evening sessions, no one sat for a minute. It was a wild scene (in a totally appropriate way), and the kids loved it. At one point I even got hoisted into the air and went "crowd surfing" (doing that only once was plenty for me).

The artist I remember most performed on the first day of that first year of the Spirit West Coast festival. She was a teenager, only slightly older than Noelle. She was brand new on the CCM scene, and so her time slot on the main stage was mid-morning. Her name was Rebecca St. James. She was from Australia and had a distinct accent that drew additional focus and attention from the crowd as she spoke about her testimony and struggles as a young Christian woman. She spoke passionately about God and about purity in dating. Her music had a depth and maturity far beyond her 17 years. Noelle was mesmerized. This young lady was clearly anointed for this ministry, and God literally showed His pleasure to us all that morning.

It was about 11:30 a.m. The sun was shining brightly, and there wasn't a cloud in the sky. It was warming up, and people were beginning to shed the sweatshirts they had been wearing to ward off the early morning chill. St. James closed her set with a moving song focused on worshipping God. As the lyrics stopped, the band continued quietly playing the alluring melody, and the young evangelist began to pray over the crowd. My heart leapt with thanksgiving that God would so abundantly bless this young lady and that we were able to bring our children to such an event. As we prayed, with hands lifted in praise, I looked up to heaven to express my heart. As I did I nearly fell backward when I witnessed a full-on rainbow appear from nowhere in the crystal clear blue sky above the stage. There was no explanation other than God smiling down on the whole event.

The fourth thing I think we did right again involved Bible reading in the home. As soon as the kids were old enough to walk, I would invite them to join me while I shaved, got dressed and otherwise prepared for the work day. Since I was gone all day and usually dog-tired when I got home, I really treasured this morning time with the kids. In addition to chatting and having fun together (the girls always chose the pink or yellow tie for me wear), I made it a point to tell them Bible stories. We had a little book called "The Bible for a Child's Eyes", which contained single page pictures each accompanied by a three or four sentence Bible story. Eventually I had them all memorized and augmented as I went along. Sometimes, while I was in the shower behind the curtain, the kids would lie on the floor cuddled with their blankets and stuffed animal friends next to the heating vent and listen as I spoke the Word into their little hearts and minds. Not only was it fun for all, I believe it had a lasting impact on our whole family. In sum, I believe including God and the Bible into the fabric of everyday life in our home was an important ingredient to the success of our family.

I wrote a poem several years ago that I found the other day in a folder of old musings buried deep in the back of our file cabinet. It is a good summary of my perspective on fatherhood and so, I thought it an appropriate way to end this chapter.

Fatherhood

Anxious, cautious, awaiting,
The breath of life,
Stillness broken with a cry of joy.

Consumed with the miracle,
Surprised by the contemplated change,
Overcome and exhausted by emotion.

Observing with gentle intervention,
Slowly gaining confidence,
To nurture, discipline and encourage.

Discovering the truth of life,
By observing through a father's eyes,
And feeling with a mother's heart.

Praying for the touch of God's Spirit,
Then a pouring,
Then a drenching.

Training up and discipling,
For them and their world,
To prepare for ultimate passage.

Playing and frolicking,
Enjoying every moment,
Each laugh, each cry, each season.
Allowing bits of freedom,
To stumble, even fall,
Then kiss and heal and strengthen.

Giving away to the Lord,
And to the other He has chosen,
To join them in the journey.

Restraining the desire to hold on,
Grieving the loss,
But knowing it is gain.

Watching the fruit of your life,
The labor of your love,

Bloom full in God's perfection.

Enjoying the quite,
The peace and reward,
The blessing of obedience.

Looking forward to the return,
The circle complete and unbroken,
The crown of jewels bestowed.

Giving thanks to God The Father,
For all He has given and shown,
Eternal family.

CHAPTER 7 - ENDURANCE

Newly married friends in our Bible study, Terry and Betsy Davis, were the owners of a small business called Tri-California. They organized and put on sporting events called triathlons. Each year in September they hosted such an event in our home town of Pacific Grove. The event was centered at Lover's Point Park and involved three sports: swimming, biking and running. The week before the event, Lover's Point was turned into a wholly different place with trucks and tents and bike racks and vendor booths and signs and orange cones and temporary fencing and portable toilets and a huge finish line structure with scaffolding. The place was abuzz with energy and excitement. For me, however, it was nothing more than an idle curiosity I would ponder as I drove by each day on my way to and from work. I mean, who in their right mind would pay money to put themselves through a grueling day of athletic endeavor like that?

Of course, we wanted to be supportive of our friends' business so we would dutifully go down on race day to cheer for the crazy triathletes. Lorrie even volunteered to help in the VIP tent, where amateur "age-groupers" would hob-nob with the professional triathletes and where event sponsors would enjoy wonderful food while watching the race from a front row seat (kind of like a sky box at the A's Coliseum). One year, Terry came up with an idea to introduce more locals to the event. It was held the Friday evening before the Saturday race and was called, "Tri-the-Ride/Ride-the-Tri". The thought was to invite those unfamiliar with the sport to check it out by riding their bikes along one leg of the bike course, which equated to six miles - from Lover's Point to Asilomar Beach and back.

Athletic activity in my life at that time amounted to the occasional beach volleyball game, a once-in-a-blue-moon game of golf and frolicking with the kids on Sunday Adventures. I thought I was in pretty good shape because I would never break a sweat doing any of these things. I thought the Tri-the-Ride idea sounded fun, so I signed up. An impressive-sized group of nearly 100 people gathered for the 6 p.m. start. For safety, and I think a touch of excitement, the pack was led along the course by an old 1950s vintage police car with lights and siren blaring. It was much like a parade.

With great gusto I launched off at the head of the throng, following the police escort and smiling all the while. But by the time I reached the lighthouse, only a mile from the start, my breathing became a bit labored, and I started falling back into the group. Not that this was a "race" or anything, but many of the people "trying-the-ride" that evening were kids and old folks, and it just didn't seem right that I couldn't keep up. The next thing I knew I was sweating ... huh? What was this? Two miles later, when the group turned around at Asilomar for the return trek to Lover's, I was in dead last place, behind every kid and octogenarian on a bike. No longer was the police car leading the group as it did on the way to Asilomar, now it was following me to ensure I made it back safely. As I approached Lover's Point, almost everyone else was already off their bike and enjoying the post-ride pasta dinner in the park hosted by Tri-California. Everyone, that is, but me. I dragged myself to the finish line and practically collapsed. It was then I realized that not sweating meant I had not been getting any aerobic exercise for years, and, if I wanted to live to see any grandchildren, maybe I should get into better shape.

Shortly after that embarrassment, I injured my shoulder playing volleyball and had to have surgery to repair a torn rotator cuff. The post-surgery rehab required a regimen of swimming, something I hadn't done since the fifth grade when I did a brief stint on a swim team. I joined that team because I was a small kid and thought swimming might be something at which I could excel. And besides, there were pretty girls on the team. Practice began each morning at 7 a.m. To get to the pool by bike, I had to leave my house at 6:30 a.m. So every morning at 6 a.m., I would rise and cook myself a hearty breakfast consisting of cereal and a fried egg on toast. The water was always cold, and the fresh chlorine in the pool burned my eyes and nose. The sun didn't usually warm things up until around 8 a.m. It was miserable, but I stuck with it.

The coach was a cranky old man with dark brown leathery skin. He wore reflective glasses that hid his eyes, and a big white Panama hat covered his bald head. He was merciless, to the point of being cruel, to us "newbies" on the team. We had to start early and stay late and clean up the locker room after practice. One morning I woke up feeling a bit light-headed but went forward with my routine anyway. By the time I got to the pool, I was feeling downright sick. I hopped into the water, but after just one freestyle lap, I got out of the pool, went to the locker room and there deposited my hearty breakfast in the toilet. When I could stand again, I stumbled back to the pool and sought out the coach. He barked at me to get back in the water and do an extra five laps for my unpermitted exit. When I explained I had left to be sick, he peered down at me through those soulless reflective lens glasses and screamed, "If you need to be sick, then you get sick on the side of the pool and clean it up later! Now, get back in the (expletive) water!"

Maybe he fancied himself as being some kind of Vince Lombardi, tough-guy coach or something, but I didn't take to the yelling and humiliation, so I left. I spent the rest of the day alternatively puking and sleeping. It was an ugly 24-hour stomach flu. The next morning, I told my folks I had decided to quit the swim team. Now quitting was not an acceptable thing to do at my house. My dad always preached that see-it-through-to-the-end-once-you've-committed mentality. But, when I explained the reason for my decision, my mother lit up with anger. She put me and the other kids in the car and drove straight to the pool. With three kids in tow, my mother proceeded to read the riot act to the coach right there on the pool deck and in front of the entire team. For the first time, I saw him soften and appear almost human. He removed his hat and glasses and apologized to my mom and to me, but the damage had been done. After all, how could I go back after having my "mom" defend me? It was simultaneously invigorating to watch my mom in action and humiliating to be the focus of the altercation. My short swim team career was over.

Getting back into the water for the shoulder rehab reminded me that I actually knew how to swim. Sure I was grossly slow and out of breath after just a lap or two, but it felt strangely good to be in the water again. My shoulder healed quickly, and I decided to stick with the swimming. I joined an adult school class that swam at the high school pool early in the morning twice a week and gradually gained strength and speed. I also decided to ride my bike more often. Rather than just puttering along with the kids, I would get up early on Saturdays and ride with a friend into and around the Del Monte Forest. So as not to miss any family time, I was usually back home before breakfast. Gradually the rides increased in length and vigor, and sweating became a goal rather than something to be avoided. I was feeling better and stronger than I had in a long time. I started paying attention to my heart rate and I began taking a greater interest in my friends' triathlon business.

The following year I volunteered at an aid station along the run course of the PG "Tri" and began getting excited about the prospect of actually attempting to do a triathlon myself. The year after that, with a lot of encouragement from my friends, I signed up for the Sprint Distance race. This was a very short race comprised of a ¼-mile swim, a 12-mile bike and a 2-mile run. I figured even I could do that. The swim was a bit daunting though because it was in the open water of the ice-cold bay and through the kelp forest, so I decided I'd better practice that.

On Friday nights for several weeks before the race, I joined a small group at Lover's Point for practice swims. The first time I didn't make it more than about 90 seconds because the water was so cold. I noticed everyone else was wearing a wet suit so the next day I went to Costco and bought a light-weight boogie-boarding suit that covered down to the knee. This helped, and I was able to complete the practice swims, but when we finished, I could not stop shivering long enough to enjoy any of the post-swim banter on the beach. The same thing happened after each session. I thought I was just a wimp and needed to toughen up. Fortunately, a friend noticed my pre-hypothermic conditions and told Lorrie about it. They recommended I get a "real" wet suit, one made for cold water ocean swimming. Lorrie surprised me with one as an early birthday gift, and it made all the difference in the world. I came to enjoy open-water swimming and the mystery of the submerged kelp forest (except for the occasional thought of "Jaws").

After completing the PG Sprint Distance event, I was officially bit by the "tri" bug. I began training on a regular basis. I joined the local gym and went every morning before work to either swim or spin. I rode my bike outdoors and ran on the weekends. I did an Olympic Distance relay (swim leg) with some buddies the next spring at an event called Wildflower in south Monterey County. Wildflower, which is known as the Woodstock of Triathlon, was world renowned and second in prestige only to the Hawaii Ironman race. The following September I did my first complete Olympic Distance race at Pacific Grove. I was all in by that time. I joined the USAT and began studying the science of the sport. I started wearing a heart rate monitor and making notes of my recovery times. I tried various combinations of food and supplements during races. I became obsessed with vitamins and fitness. I read everything I could get my hands on about the sport and even took the family to Hawaii to volunteer at the Ironman World Championships.

After a race at Treasure Island in San Francisco on my 42nd birthday, the family went into the city to enjoy an afternoon along the water front near the Pier 39 shops. We parked on a main street. My bike along with Grant's (who had also started racing) was securely locked to a bike rack on the back of our van. We were gone from the vehicle less than two hours. When we returned, the bikes had been stolen. They were never recovered, but with the insurance proceeds I was able to buy a new bike, a faster bike. Cycling speed was important to me because I was a below average runner.

A few months later I began training for my first Wildflower Olympic Distance race. This feat would require some serious training because, unlike the PG course and others I had raced, Wildflower was infamous for its hills and its heat. So, I started doing long, hot rides in Carmel Valley and in an area called the Pastures of Heaven. I looked for the steepest hills I could find. One such hill in Pebble Beach was called Spyglass Hill Road. It was one-half mile straight up that would make even the most seasoned rider strain out of the saddle until their quads and calves burned and their lungs felt like they would burst. My practice was to do "hill repeats" on Spyglass: up and down several times until I could hardly stay upright on the bike.

A week before our 20th wedding anniversary and a long planned celebratory Caribbean Cruise, and a day before Noelle's 16th birthday, I headed out at 6 a.m. with my good friend and law partner Mark Cameron (whom I had coaxed into joining me in the tri game) for some early morning hill repeats. It was a classic coastal morning, crisp, breezy and foggy. I was still exploring the speed of my new stead on the downhill portion of the hill repeats. Spyglass Hill Road has a tricky snaking curve at the bottom, near where rumble strips were placed for a golf cart crossing. Also at that location was a manhole cover and a partial bike lane along the road edge that had been eroded by recent heavy rains so that the edge of the pavement was jagged. As I went flying down the hill into the snake curve, I lost control of the bike. I'm not sure what speed I was going, but whatever it was, it was too fast. In the time it takes to blink an eye, I knew I was going down.

I had seen some very ugly "road rashes" on cyclists who had laid it down on pavement and knew they were excruciatingly painful and took months to heal. At the jagged edge of the road, the topography fell off about eight feet down a fairly steep sand hill and into a dune. In the split second I had to make a decision, falling down onto the sand seemed far preferable to skidding on the pavement and shredding my skin and muscle down to the bone. So, off the edge toward the sand I went. What I hadn't anticipated was that as soon as my front tire hit the sand it froze and my speed combined with the down-sloping dune caused the bike to flip over. I flew out and over the embankment upside down and landed on my head 40 feet from the road edge. Upon impact I felt a sharp electrical buzz shoot through my entire body. I knew I was in trouble, and as I lay there, I cried out to Jesus, like Peter sinking in the Sea of Galilee, "Lord, help!"

Mark was riding behind me and saw it all happen. I think he may have been more emotionally traumatized by what he saw than I had been by the actual fall. Fortunately, I had read a newspaper account a week earlier about a skier who injured his neck in a fall. They said if he had tried to walk away he might have been paralyzed. Not knowing the nature or extent of my injury, I decided to heed what I had read and so I just lay there, continuously wiggling my hands and feet to assure myself I would be okay.

After checking on me, Mark collected himself and went to a nearby house to phone for help. The house was owned by an elderly widow, and Mark was greeted by a menacing-looking German shepherd that kept his huge jaw wrapped around Mark's calf, poised to bite through it, the whole time Mark chatted with the kind lady. He called an ambulance. I had agreed to lay still (not that I had much choice in the matter) provided Mark assure me there would be no sirens. There were sirens. It seemed as if the entire fire department and several paramedic crews all arrived simultaneously. I was strapped to a back board and whisked up to our local hospital. In the emergency room they cut off my cycling jersey and proceeded to do all manner of tests on me. The pain was intense but endurable because my adrenaline was pumping overtime.

I was hoping it was just a sprain, something I could recover from quickly, but then the news came. The doctor approached with a pensive look on his face and reported that I had broken my neck at the C-2 vertebra. I didn't know exactly what this meant, but it sounded serious. I later learned it was the same break suffered by Christopher Reeves when he fell from his horse at an equestrian event a few years earlier. Reeves became a quadriplegic. I also learned that historically this particular break was called the "hangman's break" because the C-2 vertebra is precisely the bone the gallows noose was designed to snap in order to cause instant death. But there I was, neither paralyzed nor dead. The word miracle began circulating around the hospital corridors. I believe Jesus caught me when I fell.

No one at the hospital had ever handled a C-2 break victim who wasn't already paralyzed so everyone was afraid to touch me for fear they might cause bone displacement that would impact the spinal cord and result in paralysis. Initially the x-rays showed a fracture but no displacement (i.e., no bone movement toward the spinal cord). I was sent home in a neck brace with strict instructions to move as little as possible. Our small family room was converted into a hospital room. Furniture was moved out, and a special adjustable hospital bed was moved in. I was on such heavy pain medication I honestly don't remember any of the details. I only know that an army of friends came to my family's aid.

The hope was that with time the fractured bone would heal, and I would recover. I was scheduled for follow-up X-rays with a local specialist a few days later. I was in pretty high spirits going into that appointment thinking I would be okay, but the X-rays showed I had suffered significant displacement in the few days since my hospital release and my spine was now in imminent danger. I was ordered to go back to the hospital again. I was immediately admitted and forced to lay still for several days while they tried to decide what to do about my condition. I could do nothing but pray ... and I did so, fervently.

I was fortunate to have both a team of doctors and a team of lawyers on my side. Furious research took place, and one of my law partners found a report about a new procedure, developed by a doctor in San Francisco, that might help me. It involved major surgery to install a 2-and-1/2-inch screw through my throat and into my vertebra to realign it and then hope my bones would fuse around the screw in the long-term. The doctor was contacted and agreed to take my case. He had performed 49 such procedures with mostly good results, and he felt I was a good candidate for success. A surgery date was set, and I was transported to San Francisco several days later. In the interim, I remained confined to my hospital bed with no movement allowed. While the novel surgical procedure seemed a good, and perhaps the only, option, it was far from a guarantee of healing. If things went awry to even the slightest degree, I could end up permanently paralyzed.

The night before leaving for San Francisco, during a fitful sleep, I awoke to the sound of a clamor outside my hospital room window. It sounded like a hundred people talking all at once. It was unintelligible to me, so I stirred Lorrie who, bless her heart, slept on a couch beside my bed every night I was in the hospital, and I asked her to please quiet them all down. Puzzled, she looked out the window and reported there was no one outside, it was the middle of the night and everything was still and silent. I fell back to sleep and didn't think much more about it until the next morning when Lorrie asked if I remembered the incident. Of course I did, and I didn't understand how she could not have seen everyone I heard speaking. Lorrie concluded what I had heard were the voices of all those who were praying for me. She believed God opened my ears to heaven in that moment so that I might hear what He was hearing and thus be assured that God was listening to the many petitions being lifted up on my behalf and that He would be faithful to answer them.

The ambulance trip to San Francisco was pure torture. I was strapped to the back board so tight that I couldn't move a muscle. The thought occurred to me that perhaps this was how Jesus might have felt while nailed to the cross. When we finally arrived in San Francisco, I was delivered to the wrong hospital. The move from the ambulance into and then back out of the hospital and then across town to the correct hospital was excruciating because I had been taken off all pain meds in preparation for the surgery. The pain was nearly unbearable, but I resolved to endure and get through it until the next morning when the surgery was scheduled. I was placed in a shared room with another back surgery patient who cried out in agony the whole night. To make matters worse, Lorrie was not allowed to sleep in the room with me. I was alone, dizzy with pain and afraid.

At long last I could see, through the small window in my room, the dark night sky slowly give way to a pink-hued dawn. My surgery was scheduled for 9:45 a.m. It would only be another few hours before I would finally be put under and get some relief from the pain. Lorrie arrived around 8 a.m., and I shared with her my night's horrors. She and two friends who accompanied us to San Francisco (Mark and another Bible study friend, Amy) had spent the night at a nearby hotel. Lorrie told me she hadn't slept much either. Nurses came and began readying me for the surgery. They poked and prodded and made notes, but I didn't care what they did as long as it got me into the operating room.

There was a large clock on the wall, the kind I remember being on the wall in elementary school. The one you stare at intently the last few minutes before the end of the school day waiting for that final bell to signal your freedom. You watch it desperately as the second-hand painstakingly revolves around the clock's circumference at the pace of the proverbial tortoise and then even slower, it seems, as it struggles to travel "uphill" from the 9 ... to the 10 ... to the 11 ... and finally ... to the 12, and then "click", the minute-hand advances forward 1/60th of the clock face. It seemed an eternity until 9:45 a.m. finally arrived. I expected a team of doctors and interns to descend and move me onto a mobile bed and wheel me away to the operating room. But no one came. Lorrie and I waited. Five, then 10, then 20 minutes passed. Finally, a nurse came in to report the doctor's early morning surgery had run into some complications, and he would be delayed. She said I had been rescheduled for 11 a.m.

I was crushed. The pain was mounting, it seemed, exponentially. I pleaded to be given some interim pain medication but the nurse was under strict orders that my system be clean lest there be any complications with the anesthesia that would be administered before the surgery. I then asked to just be put out with anesthesia now, but that request was also denied. I was helpless to change my situation and near hopeless in my circumstance. Lorrie held my hand and prayed with me. Eventually I drifted off to sleep. I awoke a short time later to find Lorrie still by my side and still praying. But for my saint of a wife, I don't know if I'd have made it through those days.

We continued to wait together for 11:00 a.m. to come. As the minutes "clicked" by on the incessantly loud wall clock, Lorrie shared with me about the night before after she was ordered to leave my side. What she didn't share, but I suspected, was that she experienced her own nightmare waiting to learn if she would be caring for a quadriplegic husband for the rest of her days. Finally, the appointed hour arrived, and, once again, the doctor failed to appear. At 11:15 a.m. we were informed by the nurse that the doctor was still in surgery, but that it wouldn't be long now. No rescheduled time for my procedure was given. We waited, and waited and waited. Lorrie left for a quick sandwich and then returned, and we waited some more. The pain was getting the best of me, and my fear and frustration began turning to anger. Not that anger was going to accomplish anything, it seldom does, but I guess it was just my base/sinful side emerging to the surface. I was losing control.

The doctor finally arrived in my room at 2:45 p.m. He looked ragged. His eyes were red, his hair was tousled, and his shoulders seemed to slump forward. With a voice vaguely reminiscent of a triathlete having just crossed the finish line, he told us he was exhausted and didn't think he should do my surgery today. He said he sent his "A" team home after the difficult morning procedure had gone six hours longer than planned. Due to the nature of my condition, the danger of my procedure, and the consequence of even the slightest error, he thought it best for his team and himself to be well-rested and fresh before going in. My mind swirled in a sea of pain and disbelief at this report. But I was so exhausted I could barely do more than utter a depressed resignation. Lorrie just sat quietly and squeezed my hand. In a small defeated voice, I asked what time we should be prepared for in the morning. Then the unthinkable happened.

The doctor very calmly, almost matter-of-factly, said, "Oh, it won't be tomorrow, I have to give a lecture about the very procedure I'm going to be doing on you to 100 doctors flying in from all over the country. We'll have to reschedule you for the day after tomorrow." The last gasp of energy I had flushed to the surface, and I completely lost my mind. I angrily lashed out at the doctor, expressing my frustration to the hilt and doing everything but directly accuse him of negligence and cruelty. He received my verbal assault patiently, apologized politely and left. And there I lay completely spent, empty, writhing in pain and embarrassed by my outburst, which everyone on the hospital wing surely heard. Lorrie's head was down, I know not whether in embarrassment herself or in prayer. I asked the nurse for pain meds and was again refused. In my haze the thought crossed my mind that perhaps they were punishing me for my outburst. I was desperate and delirious.

Blessed sleep finally came. When I awoke Lorrie was gone, and I was again alone in my darkness. The glow from the monitoring machines hooked up to me was sufficient to illuminate the face of my tormentor, the wall-clock; just enough for me to see that it was 1:45 a.m. At least several hours had passed. As I lay there, my spirit cried out in repentance to God for my outburst. I don't know what had possessed me to attack the very man in whose hands my fragile existence would soon be placed. I thought again about Jesus on the cross. Of course, I knew my agony was not even in the same sphere as His, when He who was sinless took on the burden of the sins of all mankind and experienced separation from God, but nonetheless my mind and body took me there. I remembered that in His moment of agony, Jesus did not lash out, accuse or condemn. Rather He showed compassion and forgave. I began pressing the nurse button repeatedly until the poor soul on night duty came in. I told her I needed to speak to the doctor in the morning before he left for his lecture. I told her it was of critical importance, and I begged her to get my message to him.

I didn't sleep any more that night but instead prayed for a renewed spirit and strength to endure. At 7:30 a.m., the doctor came into the room, saying he had received the nurse's message from me. I thanked him for coming and with all the sincerity and contriteness I could muster I apologized to him for my outburst, and I tried to explain my revelation from the night before. I tried to share my testimony and the importance of Jesus in my life. I suppose I rambled on for about three or four minutes. With seemingly no emotion, the doctor placed his hand on my knee and simply said, "I understand. I'll see you in the morning," and he left. I didn't know whether he had really understood what I was trying to convey, but I knew in my heart I had done the right thing. I was buoyed and somehow able to get through the next 24 hours with comparative ease. Lorrie and our friends visited with me for most of the day. Numbness and utter exhaustion enabled me to sleep reasonably well that night and the next morning they finally wheeled me out of the room toward the surgical wing.

After being thoroughly prepped, I was parked on a gurney just short of the operating room and left in a cold, stark, white hallway, directly underneath a painfully bright light. I had already said goodbye to Lorrie, and so I just lay there, alone, for five minutes. During that time, I collected my thoughts about all that had transpired over the preceding two weeks and gave thanks. Thanks that God was with me. Thanks for being alive. Thanks for not being paralyzed. Thanks for my wife and family. Thanks for the many friends who had come to our rescue. Thanks for the new medical procedure that might heal me. For the first time since the accident, I was at peace. There was absolutely nothing I could do for myself at that moment, yet I was at peace, trusting God to care for me. Complete release to God is something I had heard about and actually thought perhaps I had experienced before, but the truth was I had never come close to the experience of reliance and trust I felt at that moment. They finally fetched me from the hallway and ushered me into the operating room. The last thing I remember was gagging on the intubation tube as it was being put down my throat.

A few hours later I awoke in the brightly lit operating room with machines buzzing and bleeping as they monitored my bodily functions. Above me and to the right was a large window I hadn't noticed when I was wheeled in. It angled out and extended over me to a degree. I could see people huddled in a room, behind thick, darkened glass, talking and looking down at me. I was later told they were doctors who had come from the previous day's lecture to watch the procedure first-hand. When he saw I was awake, my surgeon came down from the room above to talk with me. He was all grins and said the procedure had been successful and that I should eventually recover with full range of motion in my neck. I would only need to rest for several months while the bone hopefully fused around the screw that had been inserted into my vertebra. He explained it was possible my body might reject the screw and/or an infection could set in, but he thought both unlikely. They moved me to a recovery room where I shared the good news with Lorrie and our friends. Because I was able to keep food down, they actually released me that same evening, and we drove home to Pacific Grove. It was a long and very painful drive but I was glad to return home after almost two weeks away in hospitals.

My euphoria about the successful surgery kept me upbeat for several weeks as I lay in the hospital bed in our family room. I was on heavy pain meds and, so was in and out of consciousness a lot of the time. I wanted desperately to work in order to convince myself I still had value, so we set up an elaborate delivery system back and forth to the office each day. I was able to work, when lucid, by phone and Dictaphone. At that time, we did not yet have a laptop computer set up at the house. Although I was somewhat productive, when I later looked back on the work product that went out during that time, it wasn't my best. I hope the clients understood. We were well-supported by friends and our church during the next several long months. I wore a "TENS-unit" 24-7 to electrically stimulate the hoped-for bone fusion. I was encouraged by a friend who shared a Bible verse from the book of Ezekiel about God breathing new life into old bones. I wrote (by dictating while Lorrie or one of the girls typed for me) an email journal about the ordeal and shared it with friends. I was, in all ways, grateful and optimistic.

The physical rehab was grueling and tedious but necessary. I eventually got out of the hospital bed and into my own bed. Next, I started using a walker to get around the house. Of course, the neck collar had become a permanent fixture. I was eventually allowed to go to the office a few hours a day. Lorrie became my chauffeur on top of everything else she was doing for me. Her capacity to care give (and give and give) was amazing. One time when she was bathing me, I broke down and cried as I confessed to her that I didn't think I would have it in me to ever return the unconditional love she was showing me.

I began to get antsy about my seeming lack of progress. The doctors and therapists were encouraged with the pace of my healing, but I was not. No surprise really. In two months I had gone from the peak of fitness (at least for me) to a mere vapor, it seemed. I lost 25 pounds, and my muscle mass seemed to be withering away. Atrophy is a very discouraging thing. I couldn't wait to get outside and start walking. Finally, the doctors conceded to my requests, and I was allowed outside for a walk, but only with my walker. I was disheartened to learn I could not even make it to the end of our block before fatigue set in. I realized it was going to take me a very long time to build myself back to health, but I was determined to do so. I was also determined to get back on that bike to prove to myself I had not been defeated. First I completed a one-block walk, then two. Then I made it half-way to Lover's Point and back. A week later I went all the way to Lover's and back. I finally got the doctor's permission to go to Asilomar beach for a gentle ¼-mile jog on the sand. A week later, it was a ½-mile jog. And so it went … a bit more, a bit farther, each day and each week. At five months post-surgery, I was almost feeling normal again, not triathlon normal, but at least a semblance of normal.

The PG Tri was fast approaching, and I wanted to somehow be involved. I asked the doctors what they thought about me trying a Sprint Distance race, but they said riding a bike was absolutely out of the question until my vertebra was 100 percent fused around the screw. I was not really able to run without pain, but I had been swimming. I convinced the doctors I could safely do the short swim on a relay team. I promised to give a wide berth to other swimmers to avoid getting kicked in the head, a common occurrence during the churn at the swim start. Lorrie was extremely reluctant to give her blessing, but I think she knew I needed the mental boost, so she agreed. That short relay swim convinced me I could return to the sport, and the goal of returning motivated me to work even harder at my rehab. Once the bones fused around the screw that held my vertebrae together so that I was "safe" again, I began riding and running. The next few months were painful and glacially slow. I often got discouraged but kept telling myself I had been given a gift - the gift of being able to walk and run - and so no matter what it took, I was going to use that gift.

Physical rehabilitation was one thing, but the mental and emotional rehab was different. I was a changed man in many respects. I learned to appreciate every day, no matter what it brought my way. I became a more grateful person. I understood more about compassion for the injured and sick. My predisposition to positivity became more resolute. I learned about the value of a hospital visit and a get well card. And I absolutely knew that my wife was the greatest human being on earth. Her patience and understanding and inexhaustible support was more than I could ever have imagined possible from anyone. She was, without any doubt, my own personal angel.

There were, of course, setbacks during my recovery and many days I felt like throwing in the towel, but I kept going, I kept pushing, I kept insisting I would fully recover. One of the reasons I was so motivated was a friend from church who was a paraplegic. I was struck with what some might call survivor's guilt. Every time I saw him, he was encouraging to me and genuinely glad I was walking, as he sat there in his wheelchair. I shared my guilt feelings with my pastor, who just smiled and said, "John, I think you should have dinner with Wayne sometime." So, a few weeks later, Lorrie and I took Wayne and his wife out to dinner.

I knew some of his story because he was (and is) extremely famous. Wayne was "the" premier motorcycle racer in the world until he broke his back in a race accident. But I wanted to understand how, after such a fall from glory and health, he could be so happy with life. As we talked, I confessed my guilt about walking when he couldn't. He seemed to understand but at the same time reassured me all the more. He told me that he wouldn't change his circumstance even if he could. When I asked how that could possibly be, he told me that his accident led him to Christ and that he would never want to change that. Wow, now that was a powerful testimony. He went on to tell me that we were both indebted to Christ but had just been chosen to serve Him in different ways, him from his wheelchair and me from my feet. My friend's words lifted my self-imposed guilt, and I was encouraged to use my accident as a witness for Christ.

The following spring, I was back at Wildflower. I did the Olympic Distance course, but rather than race, I "toured". After the accident, I promised Lorrie I would never again go faster than 30 miles per hour on the bike, and that I would be diligent to wear out my brake pads on descents. I also promised her I would have a new attitude about the sport altogether. Not that I was ever strong enough or fast enough to truly compete at racing, but thoughts of personal-best times and even competition between friends was going to be a thing of the past. I even convinced Mark to tour "with" me. We would wait for each other in Transition 1 (between the swim and the bike) and then ride together, run together and cross the finish line together. The only goals were to enjoy health and fitness and be safe. Although completing the Wildflower Olympic event confirmed to me that I had regained my form, I was strangely dissatisfied. I didn't really have anything more to prove to myself, but I wanted to do more than just "get back on the horse". Since I had promised not to go faster, I decided I would go longer.

Tri-California put on two "long course" races each year. A long course, as the name suggests, is something longer than the Olympic distance but shorter than the Ironman distance. There are several kinds of long courses. The most common is the Half-Ironman distance: 1.2-mile swim; 56-mile bike; 13.1-mile run. The Wildflower weekend included such a "Half" (as they are called) but because of the extreme course conditions, namely heat and hills, Wildflower is considered in the age-group circle to be more like a three-quarter Ironman. The other long course Tri-California hosted was called Escape from Alcatraz. The highlight of that event was the 1.5-mile swim from Alcatraz Island in the middle of San Francisco Bay to Marina Green Shoreline Park in the city. The bike distance at Alcatraz was actually a bit shorter than the Olympic Distance, though the

San Francisco hills are pretty severe. The run is 8 miles and includes the intimidating "Sand Ladder" at the north end of Baker Beach. I decided I'd try Alcatraz first since my swimming was strongest after the accident.

I spent hour upon hour in the pool and eventually got my distance up to the Ironman length of 2.4 miles. Mark took a spill of his own on the bike and suffered some moderate road rash so was taking a break from triathlons when Alcatraz came up on the schedule, so I did it with my "Tri"-friend, Betsy Davis. The morning of race day, we went down to the wharf area to board a transport boat that took us across the bay to "The Rock" for the start. The boat was wall-to-wall neoprene wetsuits and Body Glide as everyone nervously awaited the famous "jump start" from the boat. There was no room to stretch or loosen up, just room to sit or stand … and fret. Lorrie would later ask, "Why would anyone want to jump off a perfectly good boat into the frigid waters of San Francisco Bay?"

As the boat rounded the historic island, its lighthouse beacon pierced the early morning marine layer. Dawn was just breaking, and a brisk breeze blew across the bow. During a pre-race seminar, we were told the key to the swim was to beware of the strong current that tends to pull swimmers west and out to sea under the Golden Gate Bridge. The advice was to aim east of the exit beach. The best landmark to use was the famous Trans-America Pyramid building in the financial district of the downtown. Being more than a little nervous and not wanting to be swept out to sea and suffer the embarrassment of being picked up by a rescue craft, I aimed even further east than the Pyramid. That strategy didn't work very well as the current ended up being lighter than expected that morning and I reached the shore a full half-mile east of the exit beach. So I had to swim west, parallel to and along the shoreline, until I finally reached the exit spot. By accidentally swimming two legs of a triangle instead one, I ended up swimming nearly two miles instead of the necessary one-and-a-half miles. Even in a wetsuit the water was very cold, and I didn't warm up until I had almost finished the bike course (riding with frozen feet was a unique sensation). I understood why convicts incarcerated at Alcatraz prison were never able to complete an escape. Without a wetsuit, I'm sure I'd have been a goner. I labored on the run, and the Sand Ladder almost did me in, but I finished my "tour" of Alcatraz and was satisfied to have completed my first long course.

I was thus encouraged to take the next step and try the Wildflower Half. I trained diligently for the next 10 months with that single goal in mind. I went to the Lake San Antonio course several times to practice riding the hills in the heat. I trained with a handful of friends, but Mark was still not yet back in the game. I missed his company as my "touring" partner. Although he had healed from his bike accident, he then suffered a serious health setback on a run and had to be hospitalized after succumbing to hyponatremia. We both discovered from that experience that hydrating with just water is not advisable because it can wash all the salts out of your system. Electrolytes and salt, I learned, are absolutely critical to long-distance racing, especially in the heat. An important part of my training involved a lot of study about nutrition (a.k.a., fueling), during the race itself. I struggled to find the right mixture of supplements. Protein powders made me gag, and salt tablets made me sick to my stomach. I search in vain for the right balance. There were innumerable opinions about the best formula so I decided to model my fueling plan after a friend, who had experience at long-course distances. The problem with that, I would learn the hard way, is that not all bodies are the same.

My training became even more intense that winter. I was at the gym from 5:30 to 7:30 a.m., five days a week. On Saturdays I would go on long-distance bike rides (50 to 100 miles), and on Sundays I would run home from church, a distance of about 8 miles. Twice a month I would do "brick" (bike then run) workouts that approximated the race distances. I think I rode almost every road on the Monterey Peninsula during those months, and my favorite run route became the Pacific Grove Perimeter (a nine-mile circle around the city limits that included cityscape, forest, beach and some extreme hills). I became stronger than ever. A week before the event, I was introduced to an experience called "tapering", which is when you slowly wean off the hard-core training so your body can recover and be fully rested for race day. That was a wonderful week indeed. I was finally ready to take a shot at my first Half Ironman distance triathlon.

In addition to the personal achievement side of it, this event was also going to be important for another reason. After law school, Lorrie and I kept in touch with several of the couples we had fellowshipped with while in Davis, including Steve and Claudia Berry. Steve was finishing his degree in accounting and then went on to get his master's at UC-Davis. We had become friends over dessert at our Americana Arms apartment. Lorrie served coconut pudding, and, to our dismay, we learned that neither of them liked coconut. But, instead of declining the dessert, they proceeded to eat it while dutifully picking around each tiny piece of coconut in the pudding. It was hilarious, and it became our story. They later started their family about the same time we did. They moved to Los Gatos after school about the same time we moved to Monterey. We had two girls, and they had two girls. Steve and I were both pursuing professional careers, and Claudia and Lorrie both stayed at home to raise the children. We had much in common and enjoyed time together. They were "fun friends". Both couples made it a priority to continue our friendship after we moved apart. Of course, living in Pacific Grove made it pretty easy for them to come and visit for "beach weekends".

Sadly, at the young age of 34, Claudia was diagnosed with breast cancer. Claudia's battle was our first close encounter with that terrible disease. With treatment she recovered, but a year later the cancer returned. After another difficult year of treatment, the disease again went into remission, and, for a while, all was relatively normal. We even took the Berry family to visit Montana with us one summer. We borrowed walkie-talkies and put one in each van so we could talk (and the kids could incessantly chatter) together as we drove in tandem the long miles through the Nevada desert and southern Idaho on our way to Big Sky Country. We all adopted talking "handles": I was Lawman, Steve was Bean Counter, Lorrie was Soul-Seeker, and Claudia was simply Red (she had beautiful wispy red hair when it grew back between cancer treatments). After that glorious trip together as families, Claudia's cancer returned for a third time, with a vengeance. It was during her third round of treatment that Wildflower was scheduled. I told her I was going to race in her honor. She was pleased to hear of my decision as it would give people an additional reason to think about and pray for her and her family. I printed up a special shirt to wear so all would know I was racing for my dear friend.

Wildflower was notorious for its difficult hills and unbearable heat. Consequently, I trained diligently for both of those conditions and was ready for them. What I had not prepared for, however, was rain. A freakish spring storm arrived the week of the race and persisted through the weekend. The night before the race, Lorrie and I lay quietly in our tent listening to the rain pour and pour and pour. I thought we might float away. In addition to the usual pre-race jitters, the rain wreaked havoc on my emotions, and I don't think I got more than two hours of sleep that night. The rain meant two things, a muddy and slippery run and a treacherous bike ride. I figured I could handle the run if I was just careful but the prospect of the bike ride was another thing. Memories of my accident haunted me that night. For safety reasons, I never rode in the rain. Whenever it rained, I just went to the gym for an inside spin instead of riding live outside. The prospect of riding on wet pavement, let alone in the pouring rain, sent shivers down my surgically repaired spine.

It rained all night long, never letting up even for a minute. When I got up around 5 a.m. to go through my race morning rituals, it was still pouring, but at least the inside of our tent remained dry-ish. The rain finally broke for a few minutes just before the race start. The race director, my friend Terry, announced two course changes due to the weather. The run course would be slightly altered to avoid the steepest hills in the back country, which were so wet no one could even stand on them let alone run on them. He didn't want any broken legs. The second change involved the bike course. At mile 42, just before the steepest incline on the course, a two-mile climb known as "Nasty Grade", there is an old single-lane metal bridge that crosses a small river flowing out of the San Antonio reservoir. Due to the slippery conditions on the bridge, Terry ordered that all riders would have to dismount and walk across the 100-foot-long platform. Moans and gripes rippled through the crowd, but those were the rules, and anyone who breached them would be disqualified. Safety was serious business with Terry.

Of course the rain was no issue on the swim. In fact, with the rain and wind conditions above the water, the lake actually felt warmer than it normally would have. I survived the start churn and eased into a comfortable swim pace. I crawled out of the water about mid-pack (usual for me) and ran up the boat ramp to the transition area to change for the bike ride. While I was in the water, the weather took a nasty turn. The rain came down harder, and a wicked wind had picked up, making the rain fall almost horizontally. The salt tabs and chunks of candy bar I had so cleverly taped on my bike handle bars had melted into a gooey mess. Sunglasses would be a no-go because they fogged up the moment I put them on (not that I would really need them that day but even with no sun they normally helped keep the wind and bugs out of my eyes). I threw on a windbreaker that soaked through in about two minutes. My "racing for Claudia" shirt would have to be covered during the ride. Lorrie prayed for me during the transition, and then together we prayed for Claudia, and then I took off.

The first mile of the bike at Wildflower is ugly with a capital "U". Coming out of the water, your cycling muscles are still groggy, and it usually takes a good three miles to warm them up and settle into a pace. But the first mile out of transition on this course forces you up a terribly steep climb called Lynch Hill. You have to get out of the saddle almost immediately and then strain the entire mile just to stay erect on the bike. The average speed must be less than five miles per hour. It was a brutal way to start a race, especially today. The rain began to feel more like sleet. Having trained on the course itself, I was well aware of this climb and so was not surprised by it. Even though this was a Half Ironman course, and consequently most of the athletes were somewhat elite in terms of conditioning, I was surprised to see how many dismounted and walked this first climb. I assumed they must have neglected to study the topographic maps of the course and had been caught off guard. "Wait until they encounter Nasty Grade," I thought to myself.

As I crested Lynch and was finally able to actually sit on my bike, I felt a momentary calm. The rain was still pounding and the wind still howling, but mentally I had adjusted and thought maybe I could actually pull this off. As I rode I prayed for Claudia. I told myself that compared to the race Claudia was in for her life, this was easy, and if she could complete that race I could certainly complete this one. I also told myself I couldn't fail here lest she might think her race was not finish-able either. I expected these thoughts to sustain me during the race, but, as it turned out, they would actually haunt me as the day progressed.

As I started the descent from the top of Lynch Hill down into the valley below I remembered my promise to Lorrie not to exceed 30 miles per hour. The temptation to cheat on that promise was enormous despite the weather conditions because everyone, and I mean "everyone" else, used the descents to make up time for the grindingly slow climbs that were around every turn on this course. I was a fairly strong climber and passed many other cyclists on the uphills, but they all screamed by me on the downs. Some even complained to me as they flew by, yelling that I was an obstacle and a hazard, and that I needed to get off the brakes and get with the program. "Dude, this is a race after all, get with it!" Seconds before the first serious downhill, at the crest of a small rise, I was prompted to look down at my front tire. I don't know why exactly, perhaps a nudge from the Lord? The tire was flat!

After the initial shock of my discovery, I carefully maneuvered to the road shoulder and dismounted. Rather than being upset, I was actually quite calm. A wave of thanksgiving swept over me because I realized that had I not seen the flat when I did, I might have had a terrible accident on the way down the first hill (even going less than 30 mph). I had changed many tires, and because this was on the front wheel, it was even easier. But what I had not done before was change a tire in driving rain. I was prepared with a spare tube and a hand pump so I went to work. The project went well until, while inflating the new tire with my hand pump, my soaking wet hand slipped. The tire was less than half full and still squishy but my slip bent the valve stem by almost 60 degrees. Because I only had the one spare tube (I wouldn't make that mistake again) and I still had 54 miles left to go, I was afraid to try to straighten out the stem for fear it might break, so I started down the hill with a less than half-full front tire. It was not good.

As I pressed on, the wind picked up even more, and the rain was now definitely coming sideways. Soon a physical chill accompanied by shivers came over me. I usually warm up on the bike after a few miles but not today. I felt like I was still in the lake, minus the wetsuit. My mind went again to Claudia, and I was glad I had not failed her by crashing on the bike. Of course, she had no expectation about my race result nor did she connect my race with her cancer battle the way I had ... no ... that was all in "my" mind. But still I couldn't let it go. Maybe I was having one of those nonsensical moments just before hypothermia sets in? Whatever it was, it kept me going mile after mile as I reached the part of the course that is on a relatively flat but busy two-lane highway. This section of the ride was normally not an issue as the farm vehicles and big semi-trucks that cruise by would tend to give cyclists a wide berth, but today no berth could be wide enough because of the spray the vehicles shot up while driving by. So, I was treated to road grime and mud along with the constant shower from above.

Although some of my "fuel" had been washed away in the Transition area, I still had other supplies in my shirt pocket and in the Bento Bag strapped to my bike. But the supplements weren't helping as planned. At about mile 38, I started feeling light-headed and nauseous. Apparently my friend's fueling plan was not working for my body (another mistake I wouldn't make again. You learn something every time you go out. This day I would learn many things). I even started wobbling a bit on the bike. So as not to become a hazard to others, I pulled over to the shoulder and rode slowly. I tried desperately to regain my wits. I came upon another guy who was about my age and had also slowed down. He was wearing an all-white rain suit that stood out like a sore thumb. Later, thinking I had been assisting a handicap-racer, someone would ask me how my "blind" friend in the white rain suit that I was guiding on the bike course had fared. I guess riding together so slowly out there on the shoulder we looked pretty strange.

To try to distract myself from my wooziness, I struck up a conversation and we talked while riding, to the extent we could hear each other over the wind (at least the rain had subsided by then). He was from Los Angeles, and this was his first Half Ironman also. We chatted for the next few miles until we got to the metal bridge. I bid him farewell as I prepared to dismount. I wasn't sure I would be able to continue. I didn't throw up, but I sure felt like I needed to. Since everyone had to dismount at the bridge, I didn't look too conspicuous as I walked my bike across the span. I'm not sure what exactly happened during that short walk but miraculously my head cleared and suddenly I was hungry. I grabbed a Payday bar from my bag and devoured it. Payday was, for me, the perfect combination of sugar, salt and protein. I was seemingly instantly revived. I hopped back on the bike and took off toward Nasty Grade.

Maybe it was because I had been riding slowly trying not to "bonk" (a term coined for passing out during a triathlon), or maybe it was the walk across the bridge, or maybe it was just God giving me a boost, but my legs felt fresher than they had all day, and I tore up the grade passing people left and right. A spot of sun shone through the cloud cover (we call that a sucker-patch in Montana), but the wind was still pretty fierce. Of course, whatever goes up must come down. The descent on the back side of Nasty Grade is even steeper than the climb, but, for most riders, it is a welcome opportunity to rest and pick up some time. It's pretty easy to hit 50 miles per hour coming down that grade, but not for me. As usual, I grabbed my brakes and began my slow (relatively speaking) downhill ride.

Then I experienced another bike malfunction. This time a loud clicking sound began emanating from somewhere on the back wheel every time I applied my brakes. No matter what I did, I could neither find nor shake the frightening sound. I became concerned it might be internal to my wheel ball bearings and that perhaps the wheel might fall off or that I might pop a spoke, which would then get lodged in the wheel and cause a crash. Visions of Spyglass Hill began nipping at the outer edges of my mind. I slowed down as much as I could, given the reality of gravity, and only braked with my front pads (not recommended on a steep hill because you can over-end easily). By the time I finally got to the bottom of the two-mile descent my hands were shaking and aching, and I was an emotional wreck. It was all I could do to nurse my failing bicycle along the final 10 miles back to the transition area. Lorrie was there to greet me when I finally dismounted. She had been worried that I had taken so long and asked what happened. As I tried to relay my ordeal, I broke down and cried.

Running was never my strong suit. I was born with a slightly deformed left foot, (injured in the birth canal) and, as a kid, I wore a brace for a while and then corrective shoes for years. The doctors said I'd never be able to wear tennis shoes, let alone running shoes, or walk barefoot. They advised I would always need corrective support. The shoes I had to wear were special order and cost my parents a fortune. I called them clod-hoppers. They looked kind of like thick wing tips. Not exactly the fashion statement a third grader wanted to be making. Somewhere along the line, the discipline about my shoes faded, and I started wearing normal shoes. Though my feet constantly ached I didn't care; I just wanted to look normal. When I started racing triathlons, not surprisingly, I had problems with my feet so I went to see a local podiatrist who took care of many of the athletes on the Peninsula. He said he could help me with some prescription orthotics. After making molds of my feet, he came back into the room with the strangest look on his face. He said, if he didn't know better he'd think my left foot had been grafted onto my leg because it certainly didn't look like it belonged. Despite the strange podiatrist humor, the custom arch supports did help and I was able to run, just not very fast.

I worked up to the 13.1-mile distance for the Half, but my time never got better than about eight minutes per mile. It was slow and steady as you go. My interest in heart health led me to a book by a famous runner named Jeff Galloway. I learned about a novel method of long distance running that incorporated short 60 second walking breaks every mile or so. The theory was the break would allow your heart rate to recover and thereby slow the onset of lactic acid build-up in your muscles. It worked like a charm for me and, believe it or not, by the end of a race I never really lost any ground on anyone else my speed because those who ran the whole time tended to slow significantly at the end, whereas I was able to keep my steady pace the entire time. This style of running also helped me cross the finish line with a smile on my face most of the time … but not this day.

By the time I started out on the run course, the sun was shining and the course was like a steam bath as standing pools of water evaporated into the sky. Coming out of Transition 2, I was feeling pretty good, mostly due to the fact I was finally off that accursed bike! I put on a fresh "Racing for Claudia" shirt and hit the trail. I hydrated and ate during every Galloway break and stayed reasonably fresh for the first eight miles. Sure I was physically tired like everyone else, but mentally I was positive. Memory of the near bonk on the bike two hours earlier already seemed like ancient history.

But mile after mile my freshness gradually faded. Maybe it was the change in weather conditions (that famous heat finally arrived), or maybe it was my faulty fueling program, or maybe it was just fatigue, but as I approached the end of the run, nearing the seventh hour of the ordeal, my legs were a mess. The final mile of the run course comes down Lynch Hill (that terrible climb at the beginning of the bike). The road is so steep you can almost fall over yourself so you really have to check your stride and reel it in. At the bottom of the hill the road flattens out as it bends to the right around a long corner. The transition area, finish chute, cheering spectators and finish line all gradually come into view, signaling the end is in sight. A friend of mine was on the course at the same time I was that day. He was doing the run leg of a relay team. Though his teammates had struggled, he was an excellent runner and he caught up with me just as we rounded that final curve.

He congratulated me on completing the course and offered to run the chute with me. I accepted and turned it up a notch to keep pace with him. When we were less than 75 yards from the finish line, I experienced what I had only previously heard about and seen a few times on television. Anyone who has ever watched Ironman Hawaii knows what I'm talking about: Julie Moss's infamous crawl to the finish line. Just as I had watched it happen to Moss, for no apparent reason my legs started to buckle. To this day I'm not sure what happened, though I think it may have been more mental than physical. Once I saw the finish line my mind just checked out and left my body to its own devices. My thoughts wandered to rest and then to Lorrie and then to Claudia and then to rest again. I neglected what some call finish line focus ... and my body just shut down.

Had my friend not been by my side, I suspect I would have collapsed and face-planted right there in the middle of the finish line chute. I began cramping and nearly doubled over. My right calf froze and shot intense daggers of pain through my body. My buddy somehow detected my distress and moved in at just the right moment to steady me. My body begged me to stop and sit, but I knew if I did, I'd never get back up. I also wanted, more than anything at that moment, to avoid having to crawl over the finish line. So, with a few gentle prop-ups from my friend, I hobbled and wobbled the last 50 yards or so and dragged myself over line. To the crowd I was just another one of a thousand who would cross the line that day. Though I may have provided a slight bit more interest, given my near collapse, I'm sure they perceived me as just another haggard age-grouper doing his crazy thing. For me, however, the finish was a triumph, for me and for my friend Claudia, and I couldn't wait to give her my finisher's medal!

I imagine most triathletes dream (at least privately) about doing the Ironman at Kona, Hawaii. I had been there as a volunteer and knew many of the pros who competed and won. Chris "Macca" McCormack was a Tri-California regular, and we chatted often. The great Scott Tinley called to encourage me in the hospital after my cycling accident. Over the years I got to know Julie Moss and Greg Welch and a host of other champion triathletes. That's one of the unique things about the sport of triathlon; the pros and age-groupers race concurrently on the same course and consequently can get to know each other. One of my jobs while volunteering at Kona was as a finish line "catcher". At first I didn't understand the job title, but I soon learned. You often literally catch people as they fall over that finish line. Then, as you usher them along you ask if they want to go to the medal tent or the medical tent. If they can't answer then you take them to the medical tent, which was akin to an international M.A.S.H. unit.

After finishing the Wildflower Half, I began seriously musing about a full-distance Ironman. However, as a father of three and a lawyer trying to build a career, I didn't see how I could possibly find any more time to train. I knew I could swim the 2.4 miles and ride the 112 miles but then to run a full marathon … I just didn't know about that. I told myself I could walk the marathon if necessary and still finish before the Ironman cut-off time of 17 hours if I could just maintain a 15-minute per-mile pace. I did the math a thousand times and convinced myself it was doable. But, feasibility aside, I decided such an endeavor would have to wait until I had more time in my life (which, for me, I figured would be at least 10 years down the road). But hey, triathlon was an endurance sport and you had to have a long term perspective on things, so I found contentment in the dream.

I did two more Escapes and two more Wildflower Halfs but I still wanted to go longer.

(I think I was becoming just a little bit addicted to the whole thing.) The morning after my second Half at Wildflower, I was grabbing a breakfast burrito and chatting with 1994 Ironman Champion Greg Welch, an Aussie from down under. Joking about my satisfaction at having completed my second Half (this one in 90-plus degree heat … looking back I probably should have accepted the I.V. at the finish line to shorten the four hours it took me to regain my senses after the race), I quipped, "Hey, maybe doing two Halfs is like doing a whole, what do you think Welchie?" With his unmistakable accent he looked me right in the eye and said, "Not quite mate. I think you still need to do a whole-in-one."

In time my body answered the Ironman question for me. After knee surgery to repair a worn and torn meniscus, I was forced to drop back to the Olympic distance for a year. That backward step cost me my fitness level, and the prospect of getting back into shape, even for another Half, seemed daunting. My kids were leaving the nest, and Noelle was about to graduate from college. I was aging up fast. Two years later my other knee started complaining every time I went for a run. I masked the pain for a while with meds and ice treatments, but eventually I gave in and went to the doctor. After a round of X-rays and MRIs the doc returned with the worst possible news. There was nothing wrong that he could fix. No repairable damage short of a full knee replacement. He said I would either have to stop running or replace my knee because the arthritis pain I was experiencing would only worsen if I kept up with the sport. Arthritis? What !? That's only for old people, isn't it? Hey, I'm barely 50. I can't be old yet, can I?

The next fall Grant, our youngest, would be off to college, and our nest would be officially empty. I figured maybe it was a good time for me to put my endurance racing career aside and make a few life style changes.

CHAPTER 8 - EMPTY NEST

During the 11 years I raced/toured triathlon, Lorrie seldom complained. My training, especially the three years I did the long courses, took me away from my duties at home a lot. Looking back, it was a selfish thing for me to do. I am fortunate to have few regrets in my life, but missing out on quality family time during those three years is near the top of my list. Off to the gym at 5:30 every morning and then working 10 hours a day left me exhausted each night. Long rides and runs on the weekends left me napping when I returned. It was an absolute miracle I was able to continue to nurture the kids and give any quality time whatsoever to Lorrie. Even when I was present physically, mentally I was kind of in a daze most of the time.

I had heard stories about the challenges a marriage can go through when the nest empties. Our marriage has a solid foundation, and I wasn't seriously worried. I knew we would survive the transition, but nonetheless, I wanted to be proactive about it to ensure all went well. Even more than that, I wanted our experience to be positive, even exceptional; something we could share with others to encourage them. For all the strength we had mustered together during our first 27 years of marriage, I knew this season would inevitably be a test of resilience.

When we dropped Noelle off at Azusa Pacific University for her first year of college, I think we all cried a bit, tears of sadness mixed with tears of joy and anticipation. Three years later when we dropped Whitney off, Lorrie did most of the crying, realizing she'd be left with nothing but men in the household for the foreseeable future. When we dropped Grant off another three years after that, I was the sadder of the two of us (saying goodbye to my son was tough on me). We've all heard it before, but it's true, there is something special about the bond between a father and his son. I was never much of a "baby" guy, but I really started connecting with my kids from about the time they were 3-years-old. The season between ages 3 and 11 was my favorite. Little boys watch their Dads closely and want to be just like them during this season. When they turn 12 and begin Middle School, the slow and sometimes painful (though absolutely normal and necessary) process of separation begins as your boy becomes a self-sufficient man.

Often as we traveled out of town when the kids were little, we would drive by an ancient oak tree alongside the highway. I always told the kids how much I liked that magnificent tree, and it eventually became known as the "Dad Tree". Then one trip, when Grant was about 5, he announced, "I want to have a tree like Dad." We all smiled and agreed that would be a good idea. As we continued east on the highway, I spied a small, lone oak tree on a distant hillside. It looked like the perfect little boy tree, and so I announced that it would henceforth be known as the "Grant Tree". Needless to say, Grant was proud as punch and thrilled to the moon. As the years passed and Grant became a teenager, however, the importance of the Grant Tree waned and by the time he graduated from high school, it was almost forgotten by everyone ... except me.

Our trip to take Grant to college happened to be along the same highway where our trees were located. The Dad Tree had sadly succumbed to old age, but the Grant Tree was still growing strong - and alone - high up on that hillside. A few weeks before the trip, I contacted the owner of the property. I told him our story and asked for permission to climb the hill with Grant on the day we would be taking him to college. The owner was gracious and gave me permission and the combination to the lock on the cattle gate near the road. As Lorrie and I were reminiscing in the car about Grant's childhood (and Grant was putting up with our sappiness), we came around the bend in the highway that brought the Grant Tree into view. I asked Grant if he remembered the importance of that hill, and, to my surprise, he got a little emotional as he said that he did. I began slowing the car and eventually came to a stop at the bottom of the hill next to the cattle gate. I invited Grant to get out of the car with me for a photo. Lorrie followed with the camera. Of course, Grant expected we'd take the photo from the roadside so he was quite surprised when I opened the lock on the cattle gate and said, "Come on, let's go." The three of us hiked the half mile up the hill to the Grant Tree, telling stories about it along the way. After a few photos, we all stood together under the Grant Tree and Lorrie and I prayed over our son and blessed him for the journey into manhood he was embarking on. Then it was my turn to get emotional.

Lorrie and I were determined not to pine after our children the way some did and we resolved not to make tribute museums out of their bedrooms at home. Instead we repainted, re-carpeted and redecorated them into themed guest rooms. Of course, the kids were (and always will be) welcome in our home whenever they desire to come visit, but we nevertheless wanted to reclaim their domains as our own. Someone once called our home the Bridges Bed and Breakfast because we entertained so many guests. Lorrie has always excelled in sharing her gift of hospitality (a gifting I, unfortunately, don't seem to have). Anyway, we decided themed rooms would be consistent with the B&B reputation, and we had a great time creating our Beach, Lighthouse, and Monarch Butterfly rooms. For Christmas one year I gave Lorrie old wooden street signs the City had replaced with more modern looking ones. The signs were for Beach Street, Lighthouse Avenue, and Monarch Lane. They hang on the walls of the respective rooms.

About the same time Grant left for college, other things transpired that made our transition to empty nest all the more apparent. First, our beloved dog of 14 years (Seacliff "Cody" - Boyhood Dream) passed away. This was a major heartbreak for me as the dog I had longed for as a boy and then finally got as a man was suddenly gone. I knew this would happen, but I guess I just didn't prepare very well for it. To address the void, within two months we got another pup. We picked him up in Southern California after a visit to see our families in Big Sky Country. So, we named him Montana. As our "empty nester" dog, we approached his training much more seriously than we had with Cody, who we basically entrusted to the kids. Not the best plan looking back. For the next year, Lorrie and I made Monday night our date night, and we took the pup to "dog school" at the fairgrounds from 7 to 8:30 p.m. Lorrie was the handler most of the time, and I sat off to the side with other dog parents on a folding chair, eating cookies and drinking cocoa. I wanted to learn everything Lorrie and Montana were learning so I could participate in the training exercises at home. After a year, the only people left in our class were those training their dogs for formal agility showing and competition. We decided we didn't want to become part of the dog show subculture so we stopped going to the classes. I think Montana kind of missed the weekly frolic with his buddies before and after class, but he got over it.

The other major change came in the form of my aforementioned knee problem. The timing of that really couldn't have been better. By retiring from the sport of triathlon, I suddenly had my mornings available. I traded in my position as a morning gym rat and instead began enjoying leisurely mornings with my wife. I still got up at the crack of dawn (long before Lorrie was interested in engaging anything other than her pillow), so I would make the coffee and bring it, along with the morning paper, up to the bedroom where together we'd enjoy the sunrise, sip our cup of joe, read, chat and watch the fishing boats head out across the bay. It was a glorious alternative to busting it at the gym every morning. I moved my workout time to noon (just for health and fitness now) and made the transition smoothly. We also developed the practice of taking Montana out for a shoreline walk each morning and hunting for sea glass on the nearby cove beaches. I think we now have more sea glass in our home than anyone in California. Lorrie still went to her Tuesday morning Bible study, and I went to mine on Wednesday but otherwise, our mornings were devoted to "us" time. My mom and dad used to refer to themselves as "us'ns". I liked that.

After our first year of marriage, a friend asked us what we thought about it all. Consistent with my classic Pollyanna perspective, I said it had been a breeze and that everything was perfect. Lorrie, on the other hand, was a bit more candid when she said it had been one of the most difficult years of her life due to all the changes she had to make in order to be my wife. I was aghast that being my wife could possibly be so difficult. Of course, she was speaking somewhat tongue-in-cheek, but I knew there was an air of truth to her comment. To make amends for the difficulties she endured that first year, I would often quip that I spent the next 35 years making it up to her. Although not entirely true, after Grant left, I was resolute to make some serious adjustments. I felt convicted about my selfishness doing long course triathlons for too long, and I was ready to make major changes. Truth be known, the changes weren't really all that hard on me; I just like to whine for effect.

Speaking of whine … uh … wine, Lorrie and I also decided to begin exploring the fruit of the vine. Several years earlier, the Davises had invited us to join them on a trip to France to watch a few stages of the Tour de France bicycle race and then to participate in a triathlon near Alsace. We planned that trip for almost a year, and things were looking positive until I researched how much it would actually cost. You see, while the kids were growing up we seldom did any significant traveling (except for car trips to Montana to see the in-laws and out-laws). The only two plane trips we ever took as a family were to Washington, D.C (the classic family trip to learn about the rich history of our country) and, in response to a gracious invitation from friends, an unexpected trip to Maui, Hawaii, one summer. We had never been to Europe and I naively planned the France trip without counting the cost. When I discovered the cost of plane tickets alone would be more than $1,000 per seat, times five, we had to reluctantly withdraw. Europe would have to wait until we didn't have three kids in tow.

While thinking we were going to France, I decided I needed to learn how to drink wine. I had been a teetotaler by choice my whole life up to that point (didn't care much for the flavor of any kind of alcohol and was too frugal to pay for it) but felt, "If I'm going to go to France, I should do as the French do and drink wine." So, I tepidly ventured out into a new world. I found that my budget could afford the "box wine" they sold at the local grocery store, and I learned that it didn't taste all that bad if it was mixed with Sprite, kind of like a homemade wine cooler (I think Bartle and Jaymes may have been on to something).

When we later opted out of the France trip, I intended to give up on the wine experiment and would have done so but for some close friends in the neighborhood who were serious wine enthusiasts. They convinced me to stay with it, and to abandon my wine coolers and join them in the pleasures and verve of finer wines. Over time Lorrie and I joined a few wine clubs, and I picked up a few books on the subject. Although the cost pinch never dissipated (the wine club's complimentary tastings helped a bit), as wine tasting gradually became a hobby, I justified the expense by balancing it against all the triathlon entry fees and bike maintenance costs I was no longer incurring. When they got older, my kids told me I needed to adopt a new hobby at least once a decade so they would have a new source of gift ideas for Father's Day (I guess I'm hard to buy for since I'm not a clothes hound). Wine, they agreed, was a perfect hobby and it has now lasted far longer than just one decade.

Another hobby I came to enjoy was gardening. For Pacific Grove, we have a fairly large lot and one of the bigger back yards in the neighborhood. When we first purchased the Surf house, I took great pride in our landscaping, and a large portion of our backyard was devoted to a swing set and trampoline area for the kids. It was classic Americana, with bark chip ground cover and everything. Sadly, during the triathlon years, my attention to the backyard seriously waned. I kept the front yard looking nice for appearances, but the back yard was behind the fence where no one could see it but us, so I let it go. The kids eventually outgrew the swing set, and the trampoline rusted and fell apart. The bark groundcover became a haven for weeds and grasses. At one point it got so bad, we had to put up a barrier to keep the dog out of portions of the backyard due to all the thistles and stickers that would get tangled in his coat. It would have been a major embarrassment had I been paying attention, but I wasn't. I was always out swimming, biking and running. Like I said, I was in a daze much of the time.

On a trip north to British Columbia one summer, Lorrie and I visited Butchart Gardens on Vancouver Island. I was overwhelmed by the beauty of the well-maintained gardens and began musing about what Eden might have looked like. I even joked that I might quit the law and volunteer to serve as a gardener at Butchart. I was smitten. When we got home, I bought three rose bushes in old pots at a garage sale and put them on our back deck. I'd always been enamored with roses, but they don't grow well in the Pacific Grove salt air. Nevertheless, I decided I would become a rosarian and strive to defeat the natural elements that worked against me in PG.

Lorrie and I hatched a plan to clear the weed patch that had once been our backyard. I opened an account at Home Depot and bought some pavers, a park bench, a dozen rose bushes and other assorted landscape plants, all manner of drip irrigation system paraphernalia, a good shovel, and gloves and we dug, quite literally, into the project of creating our own version of Butchart! It was a terribly slow process but hey, it was supposed to be a "hobby".

Our house and yard sit on a shelf of granite rock. As we experienced the year Grant was born, this was good in terms of earthquake protection, but it was not very conducive to a garden. So, we adapted. We focused on plants that thrived locally such as nasturtium (weeds in PG but coveted plants elsewhere), golden poppies and wild mint. We kept all the roses in large pots buried partially in the ground. We discovered plants called Evening Primrose and Butterfly orchids, which mysteriously grew to mutant proportions in our yard so we let them go where they wanted. Our vision of a Butchart-like manicured English garden gave way to a more natural garden-scape, which combined selected ornamental flowers amongst the wild things that, for whatever reason, liked our back yard.

Eventually we got to a point where we spent less time planting than we did just moving things around and thinning things out to create a most unique setting. The smaller granite boulders we were able to unearth became path markers, and those we couldn't budge became "features" in the garden. Over time we added a fountain, a sundial with up-lighting, a rose trellis, a glass reflection ball, an antique iron courting bench, a redwood glider, a spinning copper wind catcher and a custom rock sculpture inscribed with a poem called "Unfolding the Rose". I sought to protect my sanctuary by creating an 8-foot-high privacy wall of Morning Glories along our west fence line. Later we added big ticket items like a spa and a spectacular rock fire pit. The icing on the cake was custom-made stepping stones with inlaid china and ceramic pieces created by an artist friend who lives in her R.V. and parks in various locations along the coast. Our garden, although not Butchart, was my own little Eden, and it became one of my passions.

The first time my mother visited our garden, she said I got my love for gardening and flowers from her dad, my Grandpa Morgan. I had fond memories of my grandpa. He lived with Grandma Morgan in the northeast section of Portland, Oregon. We visited them every year when I was a boy. They lived in a tiny little two-bedroom house near a park with magnificent trees and a kids' wading pool. I adored their humble house, which to me, as a little boy, seemed like a glorious Victorian mansion.

I remember everything about that old house. It had the most unique smell about it. It smelled … old. And it creaked. There was a mysterious door on the right side of the tiny back hallway that connected the two cubby-hole-sized bedrooms, which sat on either side of the white-subway-tile-with-Pepto-Bismal-pink-accents bathroom. That mystery door led to a secret staircase (of course everything was mysterious and secretive to an inquisitive little boy). Seventeen grey-painted wooden stairs led up to an attic. I learned the fourth step from the bottom had a peculiar creak that, when stepped on, would sound an alarm to whoever (or whatever) might lurk above.

In later years a portion of the attic was cleaned out and given a fresh coat of paint to make extra space for our family of five to sleep when we visited. It was not fancy mind you, just a whitewashed room with a window at one end for ventilation. It was barely large enough for two standard twin beds, a fold-out cot (which I claimed as my own), and a tiny sink in the corner for brushing teeth. The ceiling was so low my dad couldn't stand up straight. For all that it really wasn't, to me it was like a grand castle tower room.

The main living room in my grandparent's cottage doubled as the entry foyer and was occupied by six things. On the wall opposite the front door was a little fireplace with a mantle upon which rested an array of black and white family photos. There were two small end tables that were home to the "TV Guide", the daily newspaper, Grandma's glasses and a beautiful covered candy dish made of white ivory-colored glass. It was always full of unwrapped hard-candy lemon drops that had been dipped in sugar. An antique chair with fancy wooden claw feet and dainty lace arm covers sat in one corner. A brown-colored television with a rabbit ear antenna was prominently placed on the west wall, and on the east wall, perfectly centered and opposite the television, was the most amazing piece of furniture in the world. It wasn't quite a chair and it wasn't quite a couch. It was a sort of glorious, gold-colored, luxuriously curving, lounge seat ... and with the flip of a special switch on the lower left side, it vibrated. When not occupied by my grandparents, us three kids would climb up on the magic lounger and, while sucking lemon drops and vibrating until we got dizzy, we'd watch the latest installment of "The Lawrence Welk Show". The only time the grand lounger was off limits was at 5 p.m. each day: when the world would come to a halt and children were ordered to be silent for 30 minutes while

Grandpa watched "The Evening News with Walter Cronkite".
Like everything else in the house, the kitchen too was tiny. Its most unique feature was an eating nook with built-in bench seats that jutted awkwardly out into the backyard space (possibly an add-on to the house) and doubled as the dining room. Thinking back on it, I have absolutely no idea how seven people sat around that table though I seem to recall a tray may have been used on occasion to extend the card table into the kitchen space. At the back of the kitchen was another mysterious door. This one led out to the backyard and also down to an underground area generously referred to as the basement.

The basement was dark and dusty and damp ... and an absolute delight! In the middle of the room was an old coal-fired furnace that had been converted to gas. In the far back was my grandpa's work bench, where I remember him puttering for hours. He was always fixing something. The only light in the place was a cobweb covered swag lamp that dangled above his bench. To the right was an ancient clothes washer situated perfectly below a secret hole in the ceiling that doubled as a laundry chute from the "Pepto" bathroom above. Laundered clothes were hung on a line outside or strewn around the basement on caddies to dry. To the left was the old coal bin, and stacks of "Look" magazines that sat next to and seemingly held up a rickety card table that always had a partially finished jigsaw puzzle on it. Adorning the wall near the steps leading down to this earliest version of a man-cave was my grandpa's favorite such puzzle that he had glued and put in a thin, wooden, dime store frame. It was a 14-by-17 inch depiction of Sacajawea leading Lewis and Clark. On another wall, an old cork dart board was mounted. I remember tearing pictures out of the "Look" magazines (with permission of course) and taping them to the dartboard thus creating human targets that we would torture with the darts. The highest point score was awarded if you hit them in the eyeball or better yet in the privates (boys will be boys). For all its glory on the inside, the most magical part of the castle was outside, in the backyard.

Grandpa was a very meticulous man, and his garden reflected it. A small patch of grass had identical trees planted in each of the corners. There was a concrete pad that was surrounded by a trellis covered with multi-colored sweet peas, and was just large enough for two folding chairs and a small table. In the back of the yard were uniform rows of colorful and fragrant flowers (lilacs and roses were Grandpa's favorites) that gradually fell away and down a gentle slope terminating at the rear fence. The narrow side yards were unfenced and contained large hydrangea shrubs. Behind one of those shrubs, next to the six-step high stoop outside the front door, was a secret little "cave" where I would conceal myself from my siblings during the hours we spent running around the house playing hide-and-seek. For all I knew, the place was Versailles, and I loved it.

Early each morning, after taking his pills, reading the newspaper and savoring his cup of black coffee, Grandpa would wonder out to his garden, glistening with dew, and kneel down to lovingly care for his flowers. Sometimes I would sneak down from our attic room early, carefully stepping over the fourth stair from the bottom, to join him. Oh how I wanted to be like my grandpa.

So, in my garden, in honor of Grandpa Morgan, I created a hidden nook in a fenced corner under a huge juniper bush. A special little iron gate guards the entrance and a small piece of driftwood hangs on the gate upon which I painted the words, "Secret Place". When they come to visit, the grandkids and I escape to the Secret Place and play together. Inside is an old wooden box filled with small toys we found on the beach while hunting sea glass. A little chalk board hangs on the fence so the kids can practice their letters. I also put two kid-sized concrete benches inside along the fence walls. On the underside of those benches are hidden, yet-to-be-discovered, hand written messages from my dad and Lorrie's dad to their future great-grandchildren … a written legacy waiting to be found.

Having successfully navigated the transition back to coupledom, Lorrie and I set out to explore all manner of new things together. One of those things was travel. As previously mentioned, we did precious little traveling while our nest was bustling, so there was quite a bit of pent-up demand. I learned several important lessons from my parents regarding travel in the autumn of life. The week before Lorrie and I were to be married, my mom's mom passed away (she was buried in the pink orchid-colored dress she had purchased for our wedding). She was a wonderful lady who I loved dearly … Grandma Morgan. My mom was very close to her mom, and Grandma's passing hit her hard. But, the fact that her first-born was getting married in just a week gave my mom something happy and hopeful to hold onto, and I think it helped sustain her through her grief.

Like my parents, my grandparents didn't have much in the way of money. They lived happy but simple lives. When Grandma Morgan died, the total inheritance my mom received was $10,000 from an insurance policy. With that money my folks decided to invest in the future of their family by securing a long-term opportunity for family vacations. It was something my grandparents had always dreamed about but could never afford. So they bought into a timeshare condominium community near Anaconda, Montana, to ensure a family vacation opportunity one week every August. It was a spectacular idea, and thereafter we got together at the "condo" almost every summer. We enjoyed golf and tennis and swimming and hiking and just plain being together. It provided a reason for Lorrie and I to get together with my siblings, Robin and Andy, which, to be honest, probably wouldn't have happened had my parents not been so intentional about it.

Since it had worked well for my folks as their nest emptied, Lorrie and I decided we too would opt into the timeshare idea for our family. We bought two weeks at the same resort in Montana. However, because when we visited the state we always stayed with family, we didn't intend to actually stay at the resort. Instead we joined a condominium trading club called Interval International. We would deposit our Montana weeks into the club in return for the right to use someone else's weeks elsewhere. The possibilities were almost endless, and we used our condo trades to travel to many wonderful places throughout our beautiful country. Of course, we always invited the kids along, and together we enjoyed family time despite living in different places.

I then took it a step further based on a conversation I had with an old man on a cruise ship in Alaska. We had gone to Anchorage to see Lorrie's sister, Cheryl, and then boarded a cruise ship for passage back to Seattle. Alaska was a truly awesome and amazing place (but that's another story for another time). One afternoon I was relaxing in the spa area of the ship and chatting with an 83-year-old man when in walked two strapping young men who referred to him as Grandpa. They had come to confirm their family's dinner plans for that evening. I asked the boys if they had met my son Grant, who was traveling with us. They said they met him briefly but were not hanging out with him because they were on the ship to spend time with their family. They then politely excused themselves and left.

I was impressed by their commitment to family over the prospect of making new friends and told the old man so. He smiled and said he was proud of the boys, but they were only two of the nine grandchildren he had with him on the ship. He was also traveling with his wife and four children and their spouses and three great-grandchildren. All combined they comprised a group of 24. He went on to share that they all got together for one week every year. It didn't matter where or when, and they tried to be flexible with everyone's schedule. With few exceptions they had been able to meet together every year since their nest had emptied 30 years earlier. He said as incentive he always paid for everything; the kids and grandkids just needed to get there. He said it took an enormous amount of planning to pull off each year, but it was well worth every minute and every dollar spent. Now this, I thought, was one of the best ideas I had ever come across.

When I left home for college I pretty much checked out on my family. Sure I went home for holidays and summers those first few years, but mentally I was all about me and didn't really think much about staying in touch with my siblings. Then when they went off to college and I got married, graduated, and eventually moved back to California, I all but lost touch with them other than the occasional random letter or holiday phone conversation. There was certainly no animus, no intent to become distant, it just happened. We didn't really reconnect until many years later, and I have always regretted (one of my other few regrets) those lost years. If we had purposed to see each other for a week each year, I know our lives would have been richer for it. So, the old man's idea of an annual family retreat really struck a chord with me as a way to help my kids avoid the mistake I had made.

I shared the notion with Lorrie, and she was in total agreement. We decided we would use one of our condo weeks for the "family retreat" and the other one for ourselves. Our kids were also quick to agree because first, they seriously love one another, and second, they naturally thought an all-expenses-paid annual vacation was a spectacular idea. It was a perfect plan, and we haven't missed a retreat yet (in fact, we just celebrated our 10th annual retreat together). Of course, the two-bedroom condo became a bit tight as our grandkids started arriving and the young parents asked that we not go anywhere too far away because of all the kid gear they had to haul. So, during this season of grand-babies, we have all agreed to retreat somewhere within driving distance for everyone and instead of using the condo, we now rent a large house (minimum four bedrooms and four baths … one for each family). We usually get a place on a lake since everyone can get their fill of beach time simply by coming to see us in PG. To perpetuate the idea even further, we have since purchased a third condo week (which we bought from my folks and was actually the original week they purchased with the inheritance money from Grandma Morgan) for the express purpose of giving it to the kids (they alternate years) so they can start the tradition of an annual retreat within their own young families. It was a kind of legacy gift passed down now through four generations. As the old man said, it has truly been worth every minute and every dollar invested.

Another lesson I learned from my folks was to travel while you are physically able. My dad worked hard until he retired at age 68. He often told me about his plans to travel with Mom and play golf everywhere they went once they retired. Sadly, within months of his retirement, my mom's health began to decline and my dad's soon followed. Travel became difficult for them, and their long dreamed-about season of adventure never fully materialized. A good friend of mine once said we spend a lifetime trying to figure out how to get on the train to success, but when we finally board it, we then realize we have no clue how to get off. Determined not to follow my parent's ill-fated footsteps in this regard, I started planning to get off the train gradually and early, so as to have time to travel with my bride while we were both healthy enough to do so.

We have also become avid lighthouse hunters. After visiting Europe a few times, you realize that American architecture can be a bit lacking in terms of history. Of course, there are a few American castles in the northeastern areas of the Poconos, Acadia and the Thousand Islands of the St. Lawrence River that served as vacation homes for the likes of the DuPonts, Forbes and Rockefellers, but those are the exceptions. A more common kind of historical architecture in America comes in the form of lighthouses, and they almost always have great stories behind them. We live about two blocks from the Point Pinos lighthouse in Pacific Grove, and when I "grow up" I hope to be a docent there. It is the oldest continuously operating lighthouse on the West Coast. Lorrie and I have driven along the entire West Coast and seen most of the stately giants that inhabit its shores. We have also explored much of the East Coast, from Florida to Maine, in search of a good tower to climb. Our tradition is to touch the ancient structure while holding hands and then kiss. Silly romance, I know, and we have many distinctive photographs of our unique custom to show for it.

We have also been to the Outer Banks of North Carolina to see the big daddy - Hatteras - the tallest lighthouse in the country. My uncle's great-uncle, J.B. Daniels, served as the keeper at Hatteras in the late 1800s and my uncle's grandfather was the keeper at Bodie Island lighthouse for several years, so I guess you could say I kind of have it in my blood. After we visited Hatteras, we tried to reach Ocracoke Island to the south but missed the ferry so instead we headed back north to see the lights at Bodie Island and Currituck. We then visited with my Aunt Edith and Uncle Glenn in their nearby coastal village of Wanchese. They are delightful folks, and we enjoyed a classic North Carolina feast of southern barbecue, shrimp, corn-on-the-cob, coleslaw, hush-puppies and sweet tea. We had hot apple pie (a la mode) for dessert. After dinner they took us for a drive around town to see the little white church, the school and the cemetery where they already have their stone in place with everything inscribed except the dates they will leave for heaven. As the sun set on the small harbor town, the sky was filled with a buzzing dark cloud … mosquitoes so thick I thought they might carry us away.

I've always felt a fondness for my North Carolina relatives (or kin, as they say in the South). There is something alluring about the simplicity of life there and my dad's roots. I've visited the site of my Grandpa and Grandma Bridges' graves, which are down a windy and rutted one-lane dirt road in a tiny little backwoods cemetery just outside of Zebulon.

My grandma's maiden name was Page. She was one of ten children and her family's homestead comprised a tract of farm land on the outskirts of Raleigh. Each year the Page family holds a reunion in a banquet room on the campus of Meredith College, where Grandma went to school. My folks attended the reunion on occasion, but I never got to go as a boy growing up. When my dad was in his 80s, he expressed a desire to go to one more reunion, but he and Mom couldn't make the trip on their own, so Lorrie and I offered to take them.

I wanted to bless my parents in this way, and I decided it would be fun to go see all the shirt-tail relatives anyway. My dad used to call them the "how now brown cow" relatives. When we arrived for the reunion luncheon, I was surprised at the welcome we received. The room was full of mostly 75-year and older folks. Lorrie and I were the youngest people there. Though I'd heard of many of them, I had only met very few. It was obvious I was related to these people, and Lorrie was a bit taken aback that my dad's 92-year-old second cousin Phillip looked exactly like an elderly me. Of course, everyone was thrilled to see my parents, but what I was most surprised by was their interest in "me". It was as if I was some kind of celebrity. Because I share my first name with my dad, to all these Page family members I was known as "Buzz-John" which is the way I am notated in the family records. Those records are very important to these folks. They had traced the Page genealogy all the way back to the early 1700s when the first Page relatives came over from England. I was apparently important in the eyes of these senior saints because I was the first-born male of the 14th generation of Page descendants born in the United States. I didn't know that or realize it was important ... but it was.

We had a wonderful time getting to know all the aunts, uncles and cousins two and three times removed. After the official lunch, my dad's cousins, Dave and Alan Page, suggested we take a drive out to the old homestead. Much of the farm had been divided and sold off over the years, and the final plot had just been sold nine months earlier. The land is located on the edge of what is known as the Research Triangle, which is kind of like the Silicon Valley of the East coast. As we drove up, accessing the area via a freeway exit called "Page Road", the remnant acreage was pointed out. It was in the process of being developed as a business park expansion of the Research Triangle. The land had been graded flat and infrastructure, streets, curbs, gutters, sidewalks and lighting had all been installed. The entire area was prepped for office building to begin with the exception of a small hill in the middle of it all which was surrounded by bright orange protective construction fencing. We meandered through the newly paved streets until we arrived and parked next to the little hill. As we got out of the car, I asked what the hill was. Cousin Dave said we were stopping here to pay a visit to the Page family cemetery.

Right there in the midst of all the high-tech development going on was a secluded and protected little cemetery. Dave explained that when the family sold the land, they reserved the right to access and care for the family plot. He said it was a common practice in North Carolina, and, as I thought about it, I realized how many similar little graveyards I had seen as we drove through the countryside on our way to the reunion. We managed to climb around the fencing and up to the top of the mound, which was no larger really than the size of a small house. Some of the stone markers had names and dates on them, but many were just carefully placed rocks with no identifying information. Cousin Dave, however, knew every name of every person associated with every rock. Some of the ancestors had been buried there for nearly 200 years. My dad was quiet as he stood there remembering the names and the past. Then the stories started flowing.

Cousin Alan asked my dad if he remember their first cigarette over in the old barn that once stood on Uncle Fab's place. That brought on a good chuckle. Next someone chimed in about the old mule cemetery down by the creek. Pretty soon all these 80-year-old men were waxing on about the most amazing tales. I just stood there, soaking it all in. As the laughter subsided, Cousin Dave told a serious story that my dad had never heard. As the Civil War was grinding to a halt in the spring of 1865, Union General William Sherman was marching through North Carolina. Food was scarce, and the troops on both sides of the conflict were hungry. When the Union Army arrived in Raleigh, they kidnapped an 8-year-old boy. The ransom demand was for information about where food and other essential supplies were being stored. The boy's name was Leroy Anderson Page and fortunately for me, they paid the ransom, and Leroy was returned to his family. Leroy was my great grandfather. Many more tales (some of them tall I'm sure) were told over dinner that night. My favorite was about the time the barn caught fire. I wondered if it had to do with a cigarette-smoking teen named John H. Bridges.

Of all the states where we've been lighthouse-hunting, perhaps the best are those in the Great Lakes region. A surprising piece of trivia is that the state of Michigan has 119 (plus or minus) lighthouses, which is more than any other state in the union. One spring Lorrie and I planned a trip out to Chicago to visit one of her high school chums named Steph, and then to travel on to Sister Bay in Door County, Wisconsin, to visit one of my law partners at his summer home on the shore of Lake Michigan. The two towns are only about four and a half hours apart if you drive directly from one to the other. But Lorrie and I decided to take the 21-hour long route, circumnavigating Lake Michigan in a counterclockwise direction. Crazy, perhaps, but we were hunting for lighthouses.

We had planned to leave Steph's house at 9 a.m. but because we were both awake at 6 a.m., we decided to get an early start in hopes of avoiding some of the Chicago area commuter traffic. Those three hours, as well as several other unforeseen "time" factors, would prove critical to the way our most amazing day unfolded. Because we left so early, we missed breakfast with our hosts and instead tip-toed out to the car. As a result, Lorrie didn't get her morning jolt and was soon desperate for a Starbucks coffee. I assured her we'd find one along the way, but when we hit the freeway the traffic was already getting heavy so I was reluctant to pull off to go looking for a Starbucks.

I convinced Lorrie to wait until we cleared the city, and we raced ahead to beat the commuters. As we came to our first lighthouse town (Lorrie had done a lot of research, bless her soul, so we had a long list of lighthouses to visit), we went out of our way to drive through the downtown looking for the precious nectar but could not find a single Starbucks. I suggested we just pull into a local café, but Lorrie insisted on having a name-brand cup of joe.

The St. Joseph light was beautiful that morning as it glistened in the sunrise. Because our meander through town from the freeway to the lighthouse took longer than expected, we decided to skip a few beacons we had on the list in order to ensure we got to the most important and impressive lights Lorrie had read about. Among them were Little Sable, Big Sable and Point Betsy. The route to the next two lights we saw did not include any Starbucks shops either, which came as no surprise really since lighthouses are often distant from the beaten path. As we continued north, we approached the small town of Holland, Michigan. Lorrie was finally willing to forego the logo coffee and settle for anything warm, so we pulled off the highway, drove into Holland and found a McDonald's.

Lorrie's friend had told us about this little town of Holland and said it was famous for its tulips. While Lorrie ordered her coffee, I stood near the McDonald's entrance leafing through the tourist information. I noticed a poster on the wall displaying amazing photos of tulip-lined streets. It urged everyone to follow the "parade route" to the downtown square to celebrate the annual tulip festival ... which just so happened to be "that" day. Being as much a lover of flowers as lighthouses, I convinced Lorrie we should make our exit from Holland via the parade route, which happened to be mapped out on the poster. Having her coveted coffee finally in hand, she was agreeable to almost anything at that moment so we proceeded along the circuitous route. To our pleasant surprise the route was lined on both sides of the street, and in the median, with a sea of various colored tulips, thousands of them. The diversion only took about 20 extra minutes and was well worth the time.

The next lighthouse we went hunting for took us into some serious back country, and we got lost several times. We had GPS on the phone but kept losing signal. We finally found the place at the far end of a road at the far end of a small town. Like all the others we'd seen that morning, it was still shuttered for the winter, but it didn't matter much to us. While climbing the towers was always fun, just finding them was the most important thing.

As we drove toward our next destination, Lorrie read to me about it from her research notes. It was called Little Sable, which in French means "Little Light". The structure was among the most famous on the eastern shore of Lake Michigan. One visitor's recollection, included in the information Lorrie had brought along, said, "When we finally saw her through the mist rising up off the lake, she was so beautiful we bowed down and worshipped." A bit extreme, I thought, but it must mean it's a pretty impressive lighthouse. It was.

We pulled up to a long, linear desolate parking lot that ran parallel to a sandy shore area. The fog was so thick, we couldn't see the lighthouse itself, but the signage made it clear we were in the right place. As we drove into the approximate middle of the lot, I saw only one other car. It was parked at the far south end of the lot, about 100 yards away. As we got out, we casually stretched our legs and then walked west along a boardwalk through some tallish, grass-covered dunes. About 50 yards from the parking lot, the lighthouse finally appeared. The mist was being whipped about by a stiff wind as we approached the beautiful structure. It was made of a unique salmon colored stone and towered nearly 110 feet above us. It was a thrilling sight indeed (though I didn't actually bow down before it). We had the place to ourselves and walked around the base taking pictures from all angles and then finally took our customary kissing shot.

Just as we turned to head back, I noticed someone waving at us from far down the beach to the south. I remembered the one other car we had seen in the parking lot and assumed it to be just another lighthouse enthusiast, but this person seemed very intent on getting our attention. As I watched the person draw closer, I realized it was actually two people, and they were both now vigorously waving at us and quickening their pace. We decided to wait and greet them. They were an elderly couple. He was a large, barrel-chested man with a craggy face and a long grey beard. He wore a Greek fisherman's cap and an old Navy pea coat and reminded me of what Santa Claus might look like when not in his red suit. She was as thin as a rail with stringy, mid-length grey hair hidden under a scarf wrapped tightly under her chin. They were locals and asked about us and why we were visiting the lighthouse so early in the year. We told them our story about how we were "lighthouse hunters" from California, visiting friends in Chicago, first time to the Great Lakes, etc.

After he told us a few short stories about the lighthouse, we turned again to leave. As I thanked him for waving us down and for his stories, the old man put his hand on my shoulder and with a gleam in his eye he looked up at Little Sable and said, "Yes sir, she's a beauty all right. Would you like to climb up inside her?" Glancing again at the huge door at the base of the tower, I saw the massive padlock securing the fortress. I said sure, that would be amazing, but how would that be possible since the scheduled opening for the season wouldn't be for another few weeks? He then smiled a yellow-toothed grin and winked at me. "True enough," he said "but I'm the keeper, and I've got the key right here in my pocket."

Lorrie and I could hardly contain our glee while the old man wrestled with the rusty lock until it finally opened. He invited us to climb the tower unaccompanied. The inside was freezing cold and dark. As we neared the pinnacle, the spiral metal staircase got narrower as the light from above got brighter. We finally reached the top and stepped out onto the outer platform surrounding the original third-order Fresnel lens. Lorrie clung tightly to my arm as the blustery wind threatened to blow us off the tower and into the lake. It was a thrilling moment for both of us. After a few more pictures, and more kisses, we headed down. At the bottom we thanked the old man profusely. He asked what lighthouse was next on our list. We said we were headed north to Big Sable, which was about two hours away. He told us that it too was a spectacular lighthouse and that he knew the keeper there. He pulled out a cell phone and proceeded to call his friend Bill to tell him we were coming. Bill reported that they had opened for the season early and would be glad to see us as long as we got there by 5 p.m. I looked down at my watch. It was just after 2 p.m. We had plenty of time. With a skip in our step, we headed back along the boardwalk to our car.

As we cruised north on the highway, I remarked to Lorrie how fortunate it had been that we had left her friend's house earlier than planned. She nodded agreement, realizing the kindness the clock was showing us. Because I got the impression from listening to the old man's conversation with "Bill", that he might end up waiting for us before going home for the evening, I suggested Lorrie give the keeper at Big Sable a courtesy call to assure him we were coming and that we were making good time. She had the phone number in her notes and dialed for the lighthouse. She put the cell on speaker so I could talk from the driver's seat. Bill picked up on the third ring. I told him who we were (the Little Sable keeper's friends) and that we were on our way. Curiously he said we'd better really hustle because he had to leave at 5 p.m. sharp to get to an important appointment in town. Looking down at my watch, I said not to worry because we had plenty of time since we were only about an hour away and it was only 3 o'clock. There was a long pause on the line before Bill came back on and said, "Uh, no ... it's, 4 o'clock here. Apparently you're not aware there is a time zone change between where you are and where I am." What?! Of course I didn't know that, who could possibly know there was a time zone difference between the south and north portions of a state. Didn't all time zone changes happen between west and east? After an audible gasp from me and a polite but quick goodbye, we hastily adjusted our watches, and I stepped on the gas, determined to make it to Big Sable on time.

Fortunately, we did not lose cell signal and our GPS led us right to the lighthouse parking lot. It was 4:45 p.m. We'd made it in time … or so I thought. As we got out of the car, Lorrie grabbed our jackets from the trunk because the wind was still blowing hard and as the sun relaxed lower on the horizon it was getting colder. Meanwhile, I walked over to the lighthouse sign. It depicted a trail map that showed the lighthouse was just ahead along a sandy trail, 1.3 miles to the north. 1.3 miles! I ran back to get Lorrie and tell her the distressing news. We would practically have to run to get to the lighthouse before 5 o'clock. Lorrie grimaced as she informed me that might be difficult because she had tweaked her knee coming down the spiral steps at Little Sable (we later learned she had actually torn her meniscus, ouch!). "Well," I said, "we've come this far, we might as well give it a go." So we hobbled down the path as fast as we could, kind of race walking as we went.

The sand was soft and uneven, making our trek even more difficult and the wind swirls blew stinging sand into our eyes. I kept urging Lorrie along and like the trooper she is (and always has been joining in my crazy adventures), she gritted her teeth and hustled along. I was constantly looking at my watch as the minutes ticked by. It was 4:55 when the top of the lighthouse finally came into view in the distance over the shifting sand dunes. Buoyed by this vision we picked up the pace. Panting, sweating profusely, and with eyes red and watering, we knocked on the door of the keeper's cottage at exactly 4:59 p.m. Bill opened the door and with a warm welcome said, "Hi, you must be John and Lorrie, you made it just in the nick of time."

Perhaps it was our haggard look or maybe his urgent appointment had been canceled, but for whatever reason, Bill was gracious enough to grant us free reign of Big Sable lighthouse for 30 minutes. We climbed up to the top and enjoyed a spectacular view of the sun falling slowly in the western sky. Afterward Bill told us the history of the grand dame and how he was a part of a group of people who volunteered each summer to serve as keeper for a month. I secretly put that idea away in the back of my mind as something to seriously consider someday as a vacation idea. We purchased a few trinkets from the small gift store that was once the parlor in the keeper's cottage. Having arrived in such a hurry we had not taken any photos outside the lighthouse so Lorrie and I then wandered around the grounds to do so. The beach was gorgeous, and the lighthouse had been expertly restored. It was perhaps one of the most magnificent towers we had ever seen.

But, as we were taking photos, a tinge of disappointment set in as I realized sunset and darkness was less than 30 minutes away. Because the long walk across the dunes back to the car awaited us, it would be impossible to make it to our final, hoped-for beacon of the day, Point Betsy. But it had been an amazing day, so the disappointment soon faded as we began to recall to each other all the perfect timing that had enabled our adventures at Little Sable and Big Sable. All the many small things (including the parade route in Holland) that led to us being at the base of Little Sable at precisely the moment the old keeper and his wife approached from the beach. And then, his call to Bill followed by ours, which enabled us to somehow compensate for the hour lost in the time zone change and still arrive at Big Sable a minute before closing. The word miracle came to mind. Arm in arm, we began our sojourn back across the dunes with a deep sense of gratitude and peace.

When the lighthouse was only 50 yards behind us we heard a vehicle approach. It was Bill. He pulled up alongside us and rolled his window down. "Hey guys, I'm going into town for some groceries. You want a lift back to your car?" Instantly Lorrie and I both recognized what this meant. Not only would Lorrie's hurting knee be given a bit of reprieve, but we might ... just maybe ... make it to Point Betsy after all! We quickly climbed into Bill's rig, and he had us back to our car in less than five minutes. We thanked him again for his kindness, and he drove on. We jumped into our car and loaded Point Betsy into our GPS. It was only 15 miles north. We weren't far from the highway, which followed the lake shore closely in this area, and we arrived at our final lighthouse of the day just as the sun was beginning to drop into the frigid waters of Lake Michigan. We raced to the shoreline side of the light, took a hasty kissing photo and then just stood there holding each other, numb and smiling into the biting wind as the great orange orb disappeared from view.

A few years later, we had a similarly wonderful day hunting lighthouses in the more remote Upper Peninsula of Michigan. We were traveling with the Camerons and driving easterly along the southern shore of Lake Superior. Our goal that day was to see Whitefish light station, near where the famous freighter Edmund Fitzgerald sank. In the late 1970s songwriter Gordon Lightfoot wrote a ballad about that fateful day that burned the incident into the collective memory of America forever. As we started our journey early that morning, I studied Lorrie's notes. Once again she had done advance research to ensure we didn't pass by anything important. On the way to Whitefish our map showed another lighthouse called Crisp Point. It was on the lake shore about 30 miles west of Whitefish, so it seemed a logical place to visit on the way. We had a phone number for Crisp Point, but the cell coverage on the Upper Peninsula was spotty. I tried the number every few minutes until I finally got through, only to be connected to a message machine.

The voice on the machine said he was a volunteer docent and asked me to leave a message that would be returned as soon as possible. A few hours passed as we continued east toward our goal. We had all but forgotten about Crisp Point when my cell phone came to life. It was a return call from the docent. He apologized for the delayed response, offering as his excuse that he was a local school bus driver and a few unruly kids had caused him unusual delay. After I explained to him our plan for the day, he asked a strange question. "So, you're headed to Whitefish, are you? Have you passed the blinking light in the road yet?" I told him we hadn't seen any blinking lights, but I didn't know what road he was talking about. "Oh, there's only one road to Whitefish and only one blinking light. You'd know it if you'd seen it." Having confirmed no blinking light sightings, he proceeded to give me directions to Crisp. "It's not easy to find, but if you follow my directions exactly, you can't miss it." His attempt to assuage my doubt was not very effective, but I dutifully took notes. Mark was driving. Mark always drove, and I was always the navigator. "When you get to the blinking light, turn left and go 12 miles until you see a small sign that says County Road 154, then turn right and go another 12 miles. You can't miss it," the docent said with absolute confidence.

The docent's call back was perfectly timed as we came upon the all-important blinking light less than five minutes later. As instructed we turned left and drove 12 miles to County Road

154. Everything was just as it had been reported, except the county road was dirt. The sky looked a bit threatening, and we wondered about the wisdom of driving our rental car 12 miles on a dirt road that could potentially turn into a mud road if the clouds opened up. But, being the adventurers we were, we threw caution to the wind. Hey, worst case, it would make for a great story.

For each mile we traveled on County Road 154 the forest became more and more dense and the road more and more narrow. About seven miles in, the road came to a very distinct fork. The docent hadn't said anything about a fork in the road. The forest canopy was so thick now that our GPS was not working and we had no satellite imagery to help us decide. My gut said to go to the right, and so we did. Fifty yards farther on, we saw a small handmade sign (about the size of a paper plate) nailed haphazardly to a tree with an arrow pointing straight ahead and the word "lighthouse" painted underneath. This was just the confirmation we needed to keep going into the darkening skies and forest before us. Thereafter the consistency of the road gradually began morphing from dirt to sand and three miles later we were traveling on a single lane of hard packed sand, not unlike the path to Big Sable. We were confronted with a new fork in the road about every mile or so but each time we were guided by a little paper plate-like sign. It started to drizzle, and the girls were now clearly uncomfortable. Checking the odometer, I saw we were 11 miles into the 12-mile trek so I insisted we see it through.

My expectations for the lighthouse diminished every mile we traveled along County Road 154. The single-lane sand path and funky haphazard signage certainly didn't help matters. We were in such a remote place that I almost thought I heard a banjo plucking in the distance. When we finally arrived at a small parking lot in a manmade opening in the forest, I was surprised to see three other vehicles had made the journey. The clouds parted and the sun actually came out. The breeze died to just a breath as we started down the only trail leading away from the parking area. Within moments we came upon a small cottage-like structure and the trail became a beautiful wooden boardwalk with ship rope side-rails run through 4-by 4- inch redwood posts. Pretty fancy, I thought, as we approached.

Just around the next bend Crisp Point lighthouse came into view. We all stopped and gawked. It had been renovated to pristine condition and was one of the prettiest towers I had ever seen. The cottage contained a spectacular museum and gift shop. As we chatted with the gregarious docent (who happened to be the bus driver's cousin) and told him our story, he laughed about our trepidation over the road and the weather. He remarked we weren't the only ones that struggled to find the place and added that most people never make it all the way because they choose a wrong fork from the dozen or so they confront. He was quite proud of the "new" signs he and his wife had recently made and nailed to the trees and took credit for our successful arrival. He then invited us to explore the beach and grounds and climb the tower if we wanted. Of course, I didn't need to be invited twice, and I headed straight for the tower.

Lorrie and I both climbed up the 60-foot-high beacon with reckless abandon, practically racing up the winding staircase. It certainly wasn't the tallest lighthouse we'd ever climbed, but the walkway at the top was definitely unique. To get outside, you had to crawl through a glorified porthole. If you then stood up on the narrow walkway, the guardrail was only about 24 inches high. Just high enough to clip your knee caps as you fell off. We sheepishly knelt down and kind of shimmy-crawled around the circumference to take our photos and, of course, kiss. Following Crisp, we saw Whitefish, which had a spectacular interactive museum dedicated to the Edmund Fitzgerald, and then Point Iroquois lighthouse. We finished the day with a stop at Old Mackinaw lighthouse, where the docents surprised us with end-of-the-day snacks. Just another one of many fantastic days we've enjoyed lighthouse hunting.

Our nest has been empty for almost nine years now, and though I don't feel much older in my mind, my body is definitely aware of the passage of time. I wonder sometimes about how I seem to be turning into my parents and even my grandparents. Maybe I was just born into the wrong era, but I'm becoming more and more old school ... even old-fashioned. Perhaps, as a boy growing up, I was overly influenced by John-Boy Walton, a television character who lived in the 1930s with his family in an old house in the North Carolina hills and fancied himself to be a writer, or maybe I just loved the seniors in my life so much I secretly want to emulate them. I don't know.

One of the things Lorrie and I now do that reflects my bygone way of thinking is we collect things. Not in a hoarding kind of way but in more of a romance-infused nostalgic kind of way. For example, when we first got married, we decided we had to collect "something" because everybody else did … didn't they? Spoons and thimbles didn't work for me, and because I didn't drink, shot glasses had zero utility. So, we settled on bells. I figured at least we could use them annually to ring in the New Year. Over our 36 years, we have collected more than 230 bells from various places we've been. A few have been given to us by traveling friends, but most represent a melodic record of the adventures we've taken together. I also collect antique books by my favorite boyhood author, Albert Peyson Terhune, the collie story writer. Terhune penned 18 books, and I have 14 of them on my shelf at home, which I still read for pleasure. I guess the boy dreamer part of me remains. I sure draw some strange looks on airplanes as I read "Lad a Dog" next to someone reading the latest from Clancy,

Grisham, or Brown. I have also taken to collecting stones and rocks from historic buildings and places, such as European castles. Of course, I don't do any damage to the antiquities. I just "clean up" the grounds by picking up stray shards of castle walls.

One of our most unique collections is our eclectic bevy of anchors. Hey, someone has to collect anchors, right? Our largest anchor was our first. When we moved from our little house on Rosemont, we left behind a wonderful neighbor across the street named Greg, who owned and operated the tug boat in Monterey Bay. In his front yard, Greg had a magnificent 1800-pound anchor from a World War II destroyer that he had salvaged out of the bay. I always admired that anchor and told Greg that if he ever came across another one like it, I'd love to know. I'm not sure exactly why I was attracted to the cumbersome piece of metal, but I've always had a strange attraction to the sea. I don't particularly like boating on the bay (after about 30 minutes I tend to get seasick) and I was never much of a fisherman (Grant inherited all the fishing genes from his Grandpa Marks). But in my mind there is just something romantic and mysterious about the sea. When

I mentioned my interest in his anchor, Greg told me his tug boat partner had one nearly identical to it in his yard out in Carmel Valley. He was selling his house, and the buyer hated it. The buyer said he'd give the crusty old thing to anyone willing to haul it away. I leapt at the opportunity and hired a mom-and-pop tow truck from Santa Cruz. All the reputable towers would not touch a job involving an anchor. For $50 they drove all the way out to Carmel Valley to fetch the thing and then dropped the rusty jewel in a place I'd made for it on the west side of my front yard. It has been there ever since. I couldn't move it if I wanted to. It is one of our favorite landscape pieces. Thus began our accumulation of anchors.

We have since purchased 10 other mainstays on our travels. Several of them came from Maine, where my sister resides. During a visit one spring, we came upon an old barn with a sign out front that read: "Treasures and Trash". The clever name piqued my interest enough to draw me inside for a look around. I came across an anchor that I thought would look spectacular in our yard. Because it had no price tag (nothing in the barn did), I asked the proprietor how much he wanted for the ballast piece. He asked where I was from and then paused and rubbed his chin. He looked me up and down as if trying to figure out how much money I might have in my wallet. Finally, after he had given me a thorough once over, he said, "Um...how about $75?" I had purchased a few anchors before this one and knew that was a great price, but because it is expected in such a setting (and was part of the fun after all) I hemmed and hawed with him for a minute. "Well, reasonable price," I said, "but it'll cost me at least double that to ship it home so we're looking at a total of well over $200 ... a bit steep for me." Not to be deterred, the seasoned dealer looked up into the sky and then said, "Fair enough. These things are heavy to ship, and California is a long way from here. But, I know a guy...."

Now, whenever someone tells you they "know a guy," your suspicion antenna should go straight up. I'd heard that line more than a few times before, and it was almost always just that, and nothing more than, a line. But then the man reached into the back pocket of his soiled overalls, pulled out a cell phone and began dialing. "Hello, Doug, this Bob at T&T. I got a guy here who needs to ship an anchor to California. Are you making a run out there any time soon?" I listened intently to Bob's end of the conversation, wondering where this might lead. Bob then exclaimed, "You don't say, Carmel, huh?" Holding his hand over the phone, he then whispered to me, "You live anywhere near Carmel?" Since Carmel was a mere five miles from Pacific Grove this seemed too good to be true, but since I hadn't mentioned where in California we lived, maybe it was true. I nodded yes. More jabber between Bob and Doug ensued, and then, "So, how much to haul a 125-pound anchor to Carmel?" "What's that you say? $50?" He looked hopefully at me as my jaw dropped. I quickly nodded yes again, and the deal was sealed.

I was told Doug would deliver our anchor to my doorstep within six weeks. As I went to pay Bob with my credit card, he held his hand up. "Sorry," he said, "cash only." Now my antenna went up again, and started flashing a big red warning sign. Right, so you just happen to call some guy named Doug who just happens to be going to Carmel and is willing to haul an anchor out to me for $50, and you want me to pay you cash now and walk away with nothing in my hand to show for it other than a hand-scribbled excuse for a receipt? I conferred briefly with Lorrie, and together we decided … why not, this is America after all and if you can't trust the Treasures and Trash guy in Maine, who can you trust? And besides, if we got taken to the cleaners, it would make a great story. So we paid Bob his $75 in cash and were told we'd have to pay Doug at the time of delivery.

Eight weeks later I called Doug, wondering where he was. Thankfully, he remembered me and our phone encounter with Bob from T&T and said not to worry, he was on his way. He had run into an old buddy in Iowa and decided to stay on for a while. He said he'd be to California in about 10 days. When I told him that was going to be a problem for us because we were leaving on a vacation and would be gone, he said not to worry. "Just tape an envelope with cash in it to the back side of your fence, and I'll pick it up when I drop the anchor." Was this another chapter in the scam? Aw, what the heck, I thought to myself, might as well see it all the way through. So we put $50 cash in an envelope, taped it to the fence and left town. Sure enough, when we got home our anchor from Treasures and Trash was sitting in the back yard, right next to the torn and empty envelope. My faith in American commerce had been restored.

Two years later we were in Maine again. It was October, and the fall colors were magnificent. One afternoon when it was pouring rain Lorrie and I decided to go antiquing. We met a fellow named White, who told us he "knew a guy" named Bunker who had anchors in his back lot he might sell to us. Here we go again, I thought. To save us a potentially unnecessary trip, Mr. White offered to call ahead for us. "Hello Bunker. This is White. I've got a collector from California over here looking for an anchor. Can I send him your way?" I appreciated the call but winced at the "collector" moniker knowing it was likely to increase the price I would be asked to pay.

We found our way to Bunker's house, which was in sore need of maintenance and seemingly leaned a bit to the right. With all the rain that was coming down I suspected the inside of the place might be a bit more than damp due to the patched roof that looked like it most assuredly leaked. I found Bunker out back in a ramshackle barn that was bursting with nautical antiques, including an impressive array of ships wheels, guns, cannons and swords. It kind of looked like a pirate's lair and Bunker fit the bill to a tee. He had small squinty eyes and wore an old crusty, oil-stained stocking cap. He sported a gold hoop earring in his right lobe and spoke with a thick Nor'easter accent mixed with a bit of a Scottish brogue ... just the way a pirate might talk. And he had a parrot on his shoulder to boot. I kid you not, a live parrot!

After nosing around the barn for a few minutes and admiring all the loot, I asked where the anchors might be. Bunker took me out back near the edge of the forest behind his house as the rain continued to pelt us. I began feeling like this somewhat resembled a scene from a Stephen King novel and that I might never make it back to the car. But onward I went, braving whatever might lie ahead. We finally got to what I can only describe as an anchor graveyard. There were more than 40 anchors of varying size and antiquity randomly strewn about in the yard, resembling old tombstones marking dead pirates' graves. Bunker kind of shuffled his feet, waiting for me to speak. I asked about the most spectacular specimen I saw, and he proceeded to tell me an elaborate tale of how it had once been on a ship his father captained and how it came to be in his possession. Fascinated, I asked if it was for sale and he said in a gravely mutter, "Oh, no, that one's not for sale, it has too much sentimental value to me." We then repeated similar conversations about two other anchors until finally I asked if any of them were actually for sale. He kind of grinned out of the left side of his mouth as he fed his bird friend a seed from his shirt pocket. He had me right where he wanted me. He had baited me like a pro, and the hook was firmly set in my jaw. He pointed out a large-ish piece of iron and told me its story. I was smitten by this man's stories and wanted the anchor in the worst way. I then asked the dreaded question, "How much?"

Just like the T&T man two years earlier, Bunker paused and rubbed his chin, while looking me up and down and assessing my net worth. He then answered with a candor I had never before encountered while back-country antiquing. "Well, if you were a fisherman, I'd probably sell her to you for $85, but since you're a collector, from California, for you the price will be, uh, $350." His voice was firm and confident and without a hint of waiver (and maybe just a whiff of sneer). I knew he could care less if I bought the anchor. He was toying with me just for the fun of it. The price was high for the size of anchor we were looking at, but knowing the story wouldn't be as good if I walked away, I shook his hand and said, "Deal! I think he was a bit surprised but pleased nonetheless.

Suddenly I was his best friend and he invited me into his house to complete the transaction. Inside the place was an utter dive, total chaos, with antiques filling almost every inch, not much different than his barn. He apologized for the "mess" as he guided me over the newspaper-littered floor. "Watch out for the bird droppings, they're everywhere," he said unashamedly. He had several more parrots inside the house that flew about freely as we wandered from room to room. He continued with his stories, telling me about a stately desk in a corner that had belonged to Alexander Hamilton and a tattered old American flag hanging on the wall with 13 hand-sewn stars on it. "That one's from 1778," he said, "one of the last of its kind." I believed every tale he told me. After paying him, I asked Bunker about shipping and he responded, "Oh, don't worry about that ... I know a guy... his name is "Doug." (and, yes, it was the same guy.)

Another grandparent-esq collection in our house is the timeless "family wall," which is home to a variety of portraits in a variety of frames chronicling the history of our little clan. We chose the wall along the stairs leading to our bedroom on the second floor of our house. At the bottom of the stairs each of the grands has a collage frame displaying their most recent cuteness. Next, as you begin climbing the stairs, is a collection of 5-by 7-inch black and whites from the kids' weddings, then an 8-by 10-inch of our wedding photo and one of each of the kids. Next to each wedding portrait is a framed calligraphy writing of the song I wrote for each such occasion. Finally, the high school senior pictures that the kids would just as soon disown, now that they're all "grown up".

Of all these, I think the wedding portraits are my favorites. The one of Lorrie and I is yellowing at the corners and just a bit blurry. We couldn't afford a professional photographer, so our "portrait" is an enlargement of a snap shot someone took. As I look at each of the kids' portraits, I'm drawn back to those special times. In each of their songs, I reflect on unique moments of their 23 to 24 years growing up under our roof. Noelle was our diamond, who dazzled her man (Christopher Jeane). Whitney was our princess, who was swept away to the castle of her prince (Jeffrey Paul). And with one kiss, Grant was off to live the dream with his bride (Taylor Nicole). Their weddings were blessed occasions and stand out among the best days of our lives together. The precise moment Lorrie's dad gave me her hand after walking her down the aisle was 11:11 a.m. Ever since then, that has been our special time, and Lorrie and/or I will one-ring call or text each other, or when we're together we'll squeeze hands or kiss as often as we note that time on our watch or clock. I noted the same moment of exchange for each of our children at their weddings and encouraged them to adopt the same tradition. There it is again ... that word ... tradition. I can't escape it, nor will I ever want to.

I look forward to watching our children develop their own family traditions and to becoming part of them. That began happening two years ago at Christmas. For the first time in more than 30 years Lorrie and I were away from home on Christmas Day. When they married, we encouraged our kids to leave and cleave, as the Bible teaches in Genesis. That doesn't mean never return, but it does mean make your new family your priority. Because we have the space, our kids love each other so much, and Christmas is so very special to us all, we still tend to gather at our home as one big family for the holiday. Of course that doesn't happen every year as now there are other sets of parents in the picture. Lorrie and I were prepared for this inevitable and embraced it. Our traditions would make way for our childrens', as it should be. So, how did we do it? We created a new tradition, of course.

Whitney's family now lives in Pacific Grove, and they were staying home for Christmas, but Noelle and Chris decided it was time for their little boy, Colton Sterling, to experience Christmas morning at his own house. Grant and Taylor were heading north to see us since they had spent the holiday with Taylor's family the year before. What to do? We decided to spend Christmas Eve at home with Whitney, Jeff and Hayley Grace and enjoy our usual traditions together, including the famous burger outing in honor of my dad, church, and driving by the lights along Candy Cane Lane. After enjoying time together basking in the glow of the tree in our living room, the Ernests retired to their home for the evening. Lorrie and I then went to bed for a "short" winter's nap. We got up at 3 a.m., loaded our sleigh with gifts and goodies and headed north to Roseville, where the Ritters lived.

There were very few other cars on the road at that time of morning (no surprise), and Lorrie and I reveled in the travel time together. We remembered with fondness many of our Christmases past and thanked God for our countless blessings of family and friends. We sang every Christmas carol and song we could think of as a full moon lit our way. It was, perhaps, the best pre-dawn Christmas morning ever. We arrived at Noelle's just in time to watch our two-and-one-half year old grandson awaken to the childhood wonder of a full stocking and presents under the tree. "Toyland", which was my dad's favorite Christmas song, is such a wonderful place. Grant and Taylor joined us later that morning, and together we all enjoyed our first Ritter Christmas.

In recent years Lorrie and I have also been blessed to travel to Europe several times. We have explored Italy, Switzerland, Germany, France, Spain, Greece, Turkey, Ireland,

Scotland and England. Fortunately, we are still nimble enough of foot to negotiate the quick on and off moves necessary to access boats, planes, buses, taxis, trains and subways. Our European adventure stories could fill another entire book by themselves: Kissing at the top of St. Peter's Basilica while a rainbow graced the skyline of Rome; hiking La via' dell Amore in Cinque Terre on the coast of Northern Italy; tasting wine in a cave beneath the ancient Brunello winery in Montalcino Tuscany; exploring the labyrinth of narrow streets in Sienna; floating the narrow canals of Venice; viewing the statue of David at the Piazza della Signoria in Florence; cycling in Orangerie Park in Strasbourg; dining on a riverboat on the Seine beneath a twinkling Eiffel Tower; riding ATVs to the remote edge of the Greek isle of Mykonos to find the Armenistis lighthouse; shopping (and getting lost) in the Grand Bazaar of Istanbul; following the Apostle Paul's footsteps through the ruins of Athens and Ephesus; peering over the steep cliffs of Amalfi; sightseeing along the French Riviera; visiting castles and cathedrals along the Rhine; enjoying fine Riesling at Schloss Vollards estate in Germany; mixing with the locals at Gaudi's Park Guell in Barcelona; walking together in a light rain along the Champs-Elysees in Paris; being transported back in time at the Chateau de Chenonceau in the Loire Valley of France; attending a Sunday morning church service at Notre Dame cathedral; learning the difference between the left-and right-bank vineyards of Bordeaux; being mesmerized by 40 shades of green in Ireland; singing along the bonny bonny banks of Loch Lomond; sampling Jamison whiskey at a pub in Killarney; breathing in the mist of the Scottish Highlands; marveling at Glamis, Dunrobin, Inverary and Hillsborough castles; walking across the famous Swilken Burn bridge at St. Andrews; standing at the spot where Joan of Arc went to be with the Lord in Rouen; strolling through Monet's garden in Giverny, France; enjoying afternoon tea at Harrods, and viewing the Crown Jewels in the Tower of London. The world is so big and creation is so amazing, I doubt I'll ever get tired of exploring it. The only thing I'd change, if I could, would be to have given a few of our healthy years to my parents so they could have fulfilled some of their dreams, too.

We are thankful for our lives, past and present, and we are enjoying and thriving in our empty nest. We are blessed that our grown-up fledglings return often to visit. I look forward to future adventures and walking hand-in-hand together with my bride into life's golden season of autumn.

CHAPTER 9 - LOOKING AHEAD

God willing, I have many more years ahead of me before gradating to heaven. Although at age 58, I am already familiar with the moans and groans of age, my spirit remains strong and healthy. Lorrie and I have lots of plans, hopes and dreams. Many of them revolve around family (as they always have), especially the "grands", as I like to call them. As I write this we have four grandchildren: Colton Sterling; Hayley Grace; Andrew John; and Mackenzie Jane. I love our grands but after a weekend with them, I am quick to appreciate why people have children when they're young.

Our little Colton (a.k.a. Colt; a.k.a. "45") is the senior citizen of the group at age 3. He is 110 percent boy and may be destined to become an athlete. He has a prodigious ability to swing a bat and a golf club (the bat right handed and the golf club left handed). He has tremendous agility for a tike and displays strength in all the other usual male proclivities (jumping, running, climbing, and being an all-around Super Hero). Colt also has a soft side though, and is often seen snuggling with his mom or his Nana … and once in a while, even his Granddad. Hayley Grace (a.k.a. PG --

Princess Grace; a.k.a. Hayes) is the lady of the group at age 2. Modeling after her CPA mom, she is totally in control, or at least thinks she is. She has five children of her own (her dolls) and dotes over them as much as any mom I've ever met (except in the manner she carries them, by one arm, sometimes dragging their little doll body along the floor). She has taken well to her role as big sister, though I think she may view her brother Andrew as just a large doll, her sixth child. Both cousins enjoy playing together and exploring the beach, the garden and the Secret Place. They also both seem to love music and are constantly maneuvering for a turn at the piano. Andrew John (a.k.a. Andrew John) is relatively new on the scene at age 6 months. It appears, however, that he may someday overtake both Colt and Hayley in the size department. The kid is huge. He is a very happy baby and is easily entertained by almost any and every thing. We all look forward to when he begins talking like his older cousins, who always manage to say the funniest things. Noelle and Chris were not certain they would be able to get pregnant a second time so Mackenzie Jane (her middle name is in honor of Chris's mom, who is with Jesus) is the answer to our thousand prayers.

Our family quiver continues to fill. We have a ways to go before we can field an entire baseball team, but I wouldn't put it past this bunch.

As my Grandma Bridges did for me so many years ago, I pray for each of my grandchildren daily. I pray they will grow up in Christ and will believe in and receive His gift of salvation. I pray they will follow Jesus and seek to serve Him with their lives and that they, in turn, will someday pass on to their children, who will be my "greats", the spiritual legacy they have been given.

Having Whitney's family settle here in Pacific Grove is something I never dared dream would happen. We encouraged all three of our children to attend a Christian college, and interestingly they all chose the same school, Azusa Pacific University. I have a tattered grey sweatshirt that says "APU Dad" on the front of it. I joke that it is my $300,000 sweatshirt. But seriously, we were thrilled all three kids chose such a wonderful university. We also hoped they would attend a West Coast school. Our thinking was that if they met someone at a school on the West Coast they might be more inclined to settle in the

West and therefore close to us. As it turned out, all of them met their spouses while in college and all have settled in California.

We never imagined, however, that any of our children would actually return to Pacific Grove because they had all been so anxious to leave. The three of them leaving was not a surprise since it's pretty well-expected that if you're raised in Mayberry, you will want to get away to the big city as soon as possible. That held true, but after five years of living in the Los Angeles area, Whitney decided she was a small-town girl after all. After an Orange County stint at the Big Four accounting firm of Deloitte, she and Jeff pulled up stakes and moved "home".

Jeff didn't grow up playing baseball. He was more of a water polo kind of guy. So, when I asked if I could help him coach Hayley's softball team when she got old enough to play, he seemed a bit caught off guard. In my mind, living in Pacific Grove necessarily meant Hayley would play softball because all young girls in our little town did. It's just what you do. But I then realized that the way Lorrie and I had elected to raise our children might not match with how Whit and Jeff will choose to raise theirs. This was a good early lesson for me to learn as a Granddad ... take things as they come and don't try to direct the path.

We have since adopted an intentionally hands-off approach to influencing our adult kids, and I think it has actually drawn us closer together. We remain very involved in their lives, but at their invitation. Rather than being Grandparents who have expectations about this or that activity or holiday, we've expressed our interest in doing such things only "if" that is what the kids want to do and only "if" they choose to invite us. Particularly with regard to church, we made it very clear we didn't want to influence where Whitney and Jeff decided to attend. Without much hesitation though, they chose Calvary and plugged right in. It has been fun watching them establish new friendships through Bible studies, just like we did 30-plus years ago.

I look forward to someday becoming more like Sal. Sal was a retired firefighter, who, along with his wife, attended Calvary Chapel for many years. Sal was the epitome of a servant. He volunteered to do almost anything that needed to be done as long as the job was inconspicuous. Sal hated the limelight and was uncomfortable receiving praise. He often arrived before church started and stayed until after it ended. He set up the chairs, swept the floors, cooked the burgers at the barbecue and turned out the lights. Sal was sort of my hero, though he never liked it when I told him that.

In the last several years, Lorrie and I have both experienced the loss of parents. There is nothing more painful than losing a loved one. But if there is any consolation, it is in knowing that both of our Dads and Lorrie's Mom, Shirley, loved Jesus, and it will therefore only be a matter of time until we see them again in heaven. Thankfully my mom is still with us. She is living in a retirement community in Maine, near my sister Robin. Of course, she has health issues with which to contend, but she remains engaged in and in love with life, and we look forward to seeing her hopefully a couple of times a year. It has been and continues to be valuable to observe our parents in their later seasons of life, knowing that we will be there ourselves before too long. We continue to learn from and be encouraged by their example.

Lorrie has concluded she would someday like to move into a retirement community like our Moms did. But I'm of an opposite mind. Lord willing, I'd prefer to grow old together in our home. Sure it's bigger than we "need", but so much of our life has been played out here in the Surf house, I would just hate to leave all those memories. And I enjoy our proximity to the ocean (less than a 3-minute walk) and our morning routine watching the sunrise, and the garden, and, and, and ... well, I just love it all. We are fortunate to have space downstairs that we can easily move into if negotiating the stairs ever becomes a challenge. I don't know who will ultimately get their way on this. Usually I say, "It's always about the girl," so Lorrie might think it will go her way. But I'm not sure on this question. Perhaps my nostalgic and romantic heart will prevail upon her? HoweverGod wills it to be in our future, I know we will be obedient to follow, and we will be thankful. In fact, I already am thankful, for I have greatly enjoyed this life thus far.

What, you might reasonably ask, could a man as blessed as I have been (and continue to be), possibly have on his bucket-list? Well, actually the list is longer than you might think. Jesus said He came that we might have life more abundantly. While I don't think He was referring to temporal things, it is certainly not beyond Him to bless us so. His creation is infinitely amazing and worthy to explore, and I'd like to continue to do so with Lorrie by my side. We'd like to travel for six months in a small RV and visit each of the lower 48 states, loving on friends and family along the way. We'll travel early in the day because I am a morning person: on the road by 8 a.m. and stopped by noon to explore wherever we may land. During our travels I hope to tell my stories to other vagabonds around countless campfires, encouraging them to know God and invite Him into their hearts. I also want to continue tending my little morsel of Eden in our backyard and to walk daily along the pocket coves near our home. I would like to remain fitness-conscious and stay reasonably active for cardio health. I would like to be a docent at our Point Pinos lighthouse and welcome visitors to Pacific Grove with a warm handshake, a smile and a story or two. I would like to continue serving my church. I would like to continue writing songs for my family and for my Lord. I would like to continue to encounter Jesus every day, learn more about Him and be transformed to be more like Him. I would like to decrease, that

He might increase. I would like to, perhaps, write a few more books. I don't know what about exactly, but this endeavor has been so much fun, I'd like to continue the practice. I would like to become a reader of children's books at our local library, and I would like to read "this" little book to as many grands and greats as I may be blessed to meet. I want to continue to "listen" to my adult children. I used to say the ages of 3 to 11 was my favorite season with the kids, but I must now admit that their adulthood is actually my favorite season. Noelle, Whitney and Grant have grown into amazing people who have become my best friends, and I look forward to learning much from them as this "young-old" man grows up and becomes an "old-old" man.